I AM OUM RY

A Champion Kickboxer's Story of Surviving
the Cambodian Genocide and Discovering Peace

I AM OUM RY

As told to
Zochada Tat *and* **Addi Somekh**

Afterword by
Michael G. Vann, Ph.D.

DoppelHouse Press | Los Angeles
doppelhouse.com

I Am Oum Ry: A Champion Kickboxer's Story of Surviving the Cambodian
Genocide and Discovering Peace

As told to Zochada Tat *and* Addi Somekh
Afterword by Michael G. Vann, Ph.D.

Text © 2022 Zochada Tat and Addi Somekh
Afterword © 2022 Michael G. Vann

All photographs and documents belong to Oum Ry's archive unless
otherwise noted, with family photos and articles courtesy of Manila Ban.
Maps by Thomas Bachrach.

Publisher's Cataloging-in-Publication data
Names: Ry, Oum, author. | Tat, Zochada, author. | Somekh, Addi, author. | Vann, Michael
   G., afterword author.
Title: I am Oum Ry : a champion kickboxer's story of surviving the Cambodian genocide
   and discovering peace / as told to Zochada Tat and Addi Somekh; afterword by Michael
   G. Vann Ph.D.
Description: Los Angeles, CA: DoppelHouse Press, 2022.
Identifiers: ISBN: 978-1-954600-07-2 (hardcover) | 978-1-954600-17-1 (paperback) | 978-1-
   954600-06-5 (ebook)
   Subjects: LCSH Ry, Oum. | Martial artists--Cambodia--Biography. | Martial artists--
   United States--Biography. | Kickboxing--Cambodia--Biography. | Kickboxing--United
   States--Biography. | Cambodian Americans--Biography. | Genocide survivors--
   Cambodia--Biography. | Genocide--Cambodia--History--20th century. | Political
   refugees--United States--Biography. | Athletes--Biography. | BISAC BIOGRAPHY &
   AUTOBIOGRAPHY / Cultural, Ethnic & Regional / Asian & Asian American | BISAC
   BIOGRAPHY & AUTOBIOGRAPHY / Survival | BIOGRAPHY & AUTOBIOGRAPHY /
   Sports | SPORTS & RECREATION / Martial Arts / General
   Classification: LCC E184.K45 .B36 2022 | DDC 959.604/2--dc23

Book Design: Kourosh Biegpour
Typesetting, editing and production: Carrie Paterson

DoppelHouse Press | Los Angeles
doppelhouse.com

Be calm, be kind, be brave.
—Yeay Puch

◆◦◆ Table of Contents

Oum Ry's Journey
childhood through emigration

1   Koh Chen
2   Kampong Luong
3   Phnom Penh
4   Tram Khnar
5   Pursat (Kok Trum detention center), Khtum Prahong, Arai
6   Phnom Kravanh
7   Battambang

After the war ends in 1979 (dotted line)
7   Battambang
8   Kampong Luong
9   Phnom Penh
10 Siem Reap
11 Svay Sisophon
12 Nong Samet (007) refugee camp
13 Khao-I-Dang refugee camp

⇥◦← Preface →◦←
by Addi Somekh

Oum Ry has lived — and survived — many lives in his seventy-eight years. In his story, we see the full range of the human experience, from the inspiring to the terrifying, from the devastating to the redeeming.

At every stage of his life, there is a new adventure. We see a young child who one day stumbles across an ancient art form and without any encouragement from his elders, finds the purpose of his life; we see the fruits of discipline and sacrifice while he strives for greatness in the ring of one of the world's most athletic and dangerous sports. There, we learn about the exploits of a rapacious champion who becomes a national hero during the peak of his country's cultural renaissance. But nothing can compare to the true horror of human depravity he witnesses through the violence and complete societal collapse in the Cambodian genocide, where we are given a sobering picture of the role fortune plays in one's life, both good and bad.

Few people will ever live a life with such extreme highs and lows as those Oum Ry has experienced. But there is something deeply important that we can all discover about our lives by reading his story. Profound and mysterious forces move us, forces that we don't create but to which we are subordinate, forces that have the power to uplift us or to destroy us. Yet despite these external forces, if we can find in ourselves the ability that Oum Ry's wise grandmother instilled in him as a child, to "be calm, be kind, be brave," we can do more than survive; we can thrive. And most importantly, we can take the pain of the past and turn it into a gift for the future.

Los Angeles

July 2022

1

◆ Father and Daughter ◆

A s we say goodbye to Long Beach, I can tell by the way
my dad is looking out of the window of the car that he is
both excited and anxious, mostly anxious. I can't blame him.

Whenever I'd ask my dad about going back to Cambodia,
he'd always say he was afraid of flying or he didn't have the
money, or he was needed at the gym — I never believed him.
I figured it just hurt too much. He had gone back once in
2004 to help a friend with something, but the trip wasn't
a homecoming. He only stayed six days and didn't try to
reconnect with any friends or family. It's fascinating to
think that at this point in his life, he has spent more years
living in the States than in Cambodia.

As we approach our terminal, it is becoming increasingly
more real for my dad. He's going home for the first time
since the end of the war. He plans to meet his son Oum Pee

and grandchildren, and a boxer friend who lived through the terrors he also saw. He's also bringing me, his youngest daughter, and we are going to write about his experiences.

Overwhelmed and exhausted from the hectic environment at Los Angeles International Airport, he looks at me for reassurance and I give him a nod, squeezing his hand in comfort as we walk inside the airplane. Even with fifty-six years between us, he is my best friend, and we are each other's biggest fans.

My father was a champion fighter and one of the most famous people in Cambodia from the late-1960s to the mid-1970s, the years of the cultural renaissance. He's a master of Pradal Serey, Cambodian kickboxing, and he was everyone's favorite, because despite his small frame, he possessed profound speed, strength, and fearlessness. He was only five-foot-six and one hundred and thirty-five pounds, but he fought and beat opponents much bigger than him. Over fifteen years, Oum Ry fought almost three hundred times and was never knocked out. He won over eighty percent of his matches. It is fair to say he was the Muhammad Ali of Cambodia.

But that all ended for him on April 15, 1975, the day the Khmer Rouge invaded Phnom Penh and pushed the entire country off the cliff into an abyss of mass executions, diseases, and famine. Of his eight million fellow Cambodians, it is estimated that over the next four years, nearly one quarter of the population died of disease, starvation, forced labor, or were killed.

After surviving what is widely considered one of the worst genocides of the twentieth century, Oum Ry moved to the United States in 1980, learned English, started a family, and opened one of the first kickboxing gyms in the West and the first Cambodian gym in America. He's lived in Long Beach, California for the last thirty-five years, home to the world's largest Cambodian community abroad,[1] where he is one of the pillars of the community. Everyone knows Oum Ry, he's called the "grandfather of Cambodian kickboxing" and he is still idolized by those old enough to have seen him in the ring or who love the sport and have heard of his legend.

Few Cambodian survivors in the United States have written their stories down or shared them publicly, though the effects from that epidemic of violence and chaos are felt rippling through immigrant Cambodian communities.

"It's up to the individual whether or not they want to tell their story," says my dad. "I cannot speak for everyone but I can only share what happened to me. I tell people, because I must keep going."

—◆○◆—

My relationship with my father is the most important thing in my life, but also the most intricate and maddening. Everything about my dad is a walking contradiction. He's complex, yet so simple. The sweetest and most respectful man to friends and strangers, but underneath there is a terrifying rage which could explode at any moment. He was never afraid to show affection nor failed to express how much he loved me, yet nobody can break me down and test my limits as much as he has. We have moments where we're able to sit in silence for a period of time, and it's pure bliss being in his presence, but those thoughts quickly disappear when he unleashes his hurt and frustration.

I was born an accidental love child in 2000, the result of my father (forever the player) seducing a waitress nearly thirty years younger in a local Long Beach Cambodian restaurant. He was fifty-six when I was born, married, with four grown kids. My mother had her own set of priorities, so he took responsibility for me and practically raised me on his own; buying me breakfast and driving me to school every day, and taking me to the gym after school as he juggled two jobs.

At the same time, he enabled a lot of crazy happenings in our ecosystem. Our house was like a cheap motel, and his generosity meant he would pick up people off the streets and let them stay at the gym. Because he is naturally altruistic, he would be financially helping whoever he could. He had empathy for anyone and everyone. But when pressure would build up, his usual response to stress was to lash out. I have come to know that this is his pain talking; I've learned to build thick skin over the years. I happen to be an easy target because I'm the closest to him, and he knows I'll forgive him, no matter what.

There's one story that encapsulates our relationship, past and present. My dad says he has no recollection of it ever happening, though he admits, "When I get angry, I go crazy and my mind goes blank." This is my version of events, through the eyes of a child who didn't yet understand all of what was happening in my community.

It was a regular Saturday afternoon, in the summer right before I turned twelve, and I remember being hungry from playing outside all day. Since my dad didn't know how to cook, he would always pick up precooked food from a local Cambodian supermarket. That day, he brought back spring rolls. I ran back home, my father gave them to me, and I took the spring rolls outside and shared them with three other neighborhood kids. All of it we devoured within seconds. Soon after, since I was still hungry, I went back inside to make a bologna sandwich for myself, but my dad stopped me as I pulled the ingredients out.

"Why are you making a sandwich? I bought you food. I know you didn't eat it all that fast!"

He has always been very quick to get angry.

"I shared it with my friends. They were really hungry too," I quietly responded, looking at the ground.

"Why?! They have their own parents who feed them! I buy you food so *you* can eat, not them!"

What happened next was quite a blur, but I remember being met with a side kick that made me fall onto my knees. He was still looking at me furiously, but I got up and gave him a hard roundhouse kick to his shoulder, causing him to topple over. That was the first time I had ever fought back against him, and he was on the ground, stunned. I had never seen him look at me that way before. I bolted towards the door and ran to my neighbors' house, where I hid the rest of the day. I knew if I gave him some time to cool down, he'd be back to normal, as if nothing had happened.

That day was one of the most pivotal points in my life. After that, his intimidation tactic, which he used until my senior year of high school, was to raise his hand at my face as if he were going to strike me, but I'd do the same back.

Any stress between us was always balanced by the sweetness of simply spending time together. One of my favorite activities to do with my dad as a child was to drive down the Pacific Coast Highway at night, from Long Beach south to Laguna Beach and back. Driving around for hours, in complete silence, made me so happy. Falling asleep in the car and being carried to bed was the best feeling in the world. I faked being asleep most of the time, and my dad knew, but he carried me upstairs anyway.

In this way, I was raised on the Eastside of Long Beach, in the heart of Cambodia Town, absorbing both American and Cambodian values. From the outside world (school and internet, mostly), I discovered the importance of individuality, curiosity, and social justice, and from my inside world (my parents and the community), I learned respect for elders and primacy of family. I grew to be some sort of cultural amphibian, slipping from one world into the other, even when the two sets of values would contradict one another.

While all children of immigrants carry the hopes and dreams of their lineage, one thing I learned at a young age is that being the child of genocide survivors means to carry the crushing weight of intergenerational trauma. When I was seven years old, my mom told me about a specific ordeal during the genocide. She had snuck out at night to steal some vegetables for her dad to eat and a soldier had found her and beat her unconscious. She was eight years old. She still has a twelve-inch scar from the whipping. "I'm sorry, Mommy," was all I could whisper to her before her wails filled the room like an alarm. From then on, I became too scared to ask about any Khmer person's experiences during the war, or even ask their kids. I wasn't sure what I'd trigger.

Without ever talking to other Khmer kids about their parents' experiences, I had always felt that mutual understanding and profound connection with one another. We understood each other through non verbal communication. I don't know when I became aware of what had happened in Cambodia. I remember thinking it was this esoteric secret I wasn't allowed to speak about. Every Cambodian person around us was a survivor and had been affected by the genocide in one way or another. It's like I've always known that our people endured hell.

The topic of death is often taboo in the Western world, but certainly not in our culture. The Cambodian people of my parents' generation experienced such an extreme amount of death in such a short period of time that it seems we have a warped relationship with it, a strange mixture of both acceptance and avoidance. As a child, I didn't understand why my dad never attended anyone's funerals. His callous way of delivering the news of someone's death didn't help either. I'd always burst into tears after he'd break the news that so-and-so had passed away, and he'd always tell me that I shouldn't cry because "the only thing life will promise you is death." I now understand he was, and still is, protecting himself. He has probably seen as many corpses as the average mortician.

Though our people don't have sit-down conversations about the Pol Pot years, the topic is always hanging in the air with some crass or cynical joke. When my mom would come home from a long day at work and I would ask her how it was, she would snap back something like, "I worked the rice fields in a bloody pool of dead bodies every day for the Khmer Rouge, I think I can handle my idiot boss." I had become numb to all the jokes that were being said around me by the elders. *If that's what helps them cope*, I thought — as they definitely weren't having open conversations about it and joking was their way of managing — *who am I to police that?*

To this day, if you ask my dad about the specifics about the Khmer Rouge and the Cambodian civil war, he'll probably tell you he doesn't know. My dad doesn't do politics, he's a fighter, or at least that's what he'd say. It was one of the many chapters of his life. He just accepted it for what happened.

—◆○◆—

I know so much about this man, and yet so little at the same time; so many details about my father's life were a mystery to me. Over the years, I heard bits and pieces of what he had gone through, but never really sat down and asked him questions. How do you survive your entire world collapsing? How do you stay sane when everything becomes vicious and absurd? How do you find the hope, or the strength, to not give up? How do you go on with life after experiencing all the horror he has?

I'm twenty-two years old, and my father will be seventy-eight in May. When I turned eighteen, I realized that I shouldn't wait to have this conversation. I wanted to know more about Oum Ry, for myself, but I also wanted the world to know. I asked him if we could meet at the gym, during off hours, to talk uninterrupted. I would ask questions, and we would record it with our family friend, Addi. In 2019, all of us met together three times a week for three months so we could have these conversations, accompanied by a friend of my dad's, Tippana Tith, who helped sharpen his memory and translated his story, with me clarifying details. I transcribed roughly sixty hours of tape that make the core of this book and worked with Addi to compose the text.

I've never seen my dad cry, but the closest I got was when we first started doing the interviews and we got to talking about his mom. He never knew what happened to her, but after the Khmer Rouge, he never saw or heard of her again. I broached the question gently about my grandmother. His eyes were red, filling up with tears threatening to pour out at any moment, but he kept himself composed.

It was through moments like this, that as this project progressed and matured, it felt natural and crucial for Oum Ry to visit Cambodia again. I told him I would go with him. We had our plans set to travel in the spring of 2020. But it would be another two years before we arrived because of a global pandemic that at this writing has already taken a million lives in the United States, and millions more worldwide.[2] In those intervening years, I had more conversations and there were realizations occurring for me all the time as I journaled and observed the father I now know and understand so much better.

"Are you okay, Pa?" We are seven hours into the twenty-one-hour journey. I have been dozing in and out of sleep the past few hours, and every time I wake, I look at my dad, his eyes puffy, glued to the window. It is night over the Pacific, and I can see his reflection. He hasn't slept yet, I'm not even sure if he's closed his eyes longer than a few seconds.

"Yes. I am okay, kaun*," he quietly responds, shifting his eyes at me for a second before redirecting his gaze to the dark and cloudy sky. That's always his response. I guess I just ask out of habit.

I rest my head on his shoulder as I notice he starts to doze off.

* "Kaun" is a term of endearment in Khmer ("k'mai"), meaning "child."

2

→ Childhood →

Let's start at the beginning. Tell me about your childhood.

I was born on May 15, 1944, and grew up in Koh Chen, a small community that lived on an island in the Mekong River in central Cambodia. There were about fifty families in my area, and almost all the people worked at a silver-plating factory. My parents worked there, engraving silver by hand into ornate vases which were used for Buddhist ceremonies.

There were six kids, and I was the second youngest. My parents always got along — I never saw them fight with each other. We had a very peaceful life at the beginning. We weren't rich, but we weren't poor either, and we always had enough to eat. Fermented fish paste (prahok), snake, eel, and pig were all common, but my favorite was turtle roasted in banana leaves. And all the kids loved eating turtle eggs, you could just crack open the top and drink it right out of the shell.

Since we lived on an island, we had to take a boat to get to school in the morning. The boat was basically a bus, usually had eight people riding and one person paddling, and took an hour each way, but it was only a fifteen-minute ride with a motorboat, which my family couldn't afford. Once we got on land, we still had to walk two kilometers to school.

Back then, we were more scared of teachers than the police. The teachers were allowed to beat the children. When writing on the chalkboard, if you got something wrong, they'd push you or kick your back. Whipping with a stick was very common — sometimes they hit the students until they bled. The worst is when they would punish the kids by making us kneel on the hard and sharp jackfruit skin.

When I was six years old, my father died. I never found out how. But then it was my mother with her six kids and my grandmother, who was my father's mother. My grandmother's name was Yeay Puch, and she played a very big role in my life.

What was your relationship like with Yeay Puch?

At night I would massage her legs and she'd tell me stories about her life — every night a different story. She was always reading, so she was very knowledgeable and wise. She had an enormous collection of ancient Buddhist scrolls, written in Sanskrit, all made out of palm leaves.[3] She must have had at least a hundred of these scrolls, and she would study them every night after dinner.

Yeay Puch loved all the kids, but my brothers and sisters didn't believe her and were not interested in her stories. But I was, and I listened to her every night. No one ever taught me as well as my grandmother.

She shared with me the famous Cambodian saying, "The rice won't bear grain if it stands tall, but it will if it bows." She explained, "Whatever you do, you must give people respect."

She also told me, "If you are humble, people will love you and you will become famous." When I was young, I didn't understand, or believe her, but as I got older, I saw that she was right. I see now that she was a psychic. The palm leaf scrolls helped her see into the future. For instance, she told me once, "Rice will one day cook itself" — which I thought was crazy until many years later when I came to America and saw my first electric rice cooker.

One night, in a very solemn voice Yeay Puch said to me, "There will be an empty city, with empty streets and empty homes." I had no idea what she was talking about, but eventually I would see it with my own eyes when I returned to Phnom Penh after the war.

By far the most important thing that Yeay Puch taught me was to honor and worship the guardian spirit from the ancient times named Ta Kaan. She told me, "Ta Kaan is the god of fighters, and he is an educator. He can teach you and help you. Pray to him every day — if you believe, he will help you. If you don't believe, he won't." Since then, I have prayed to Ta Kaan every day of my life. There are so many times where I should have been killed, too many to count, and there were so many miracles, that I believe my grandmother and Ta Kaan have helped me survive.

When I was seven, Yeay Puch passed away at the age of eighty-three. I shaved my head and lived with the monks for three days to pay my respect to her. She was like a god to me and years later, every time I would go up to fight, I would think about my grandmother and follow her advice, "Be calm, be kind, be brave." And to this day, because of my grandmother, I am not afraid of anybody.

When my grandmother died, then it was just my mom to take care of us and she decided we should sell the house and move. Because my oldest brother was studying to pass his certificate to become a college professor, we moved from our island to Kampong Luong in the province of Kandal.

How did you adjust to your new community?

At our new home, I quickly became friends with a boy who lived across the street named Sarith Ban. I was eight years old and he was six. His family also worked in silvering, and his father had also died when Sarith was very young. We quickly became best friends and did everything together.

During summer vacation, Sarith and I used to sell bread to make money. A popular snack in our province was a Cambodian bread called nom pang, which is eaten with sugar and condensed milk. We would get up at four a.m. to go to the bakery and buy one hundred pieces of bread for sixty riel. Then we walked or biked around all day and when people wanted to buy some, we would slice open the bread and add sugar and condensed milk. We would make back our investment plus sixty riel for ourselves at the end of the day.

Sarith and I were inseparable, and after the war, it was Sarith who offered to sponsor my arrival to America. To this day, almost seventy years later, we are still best friends, and only live a few miles from each other.

As I got older, I began to notice that we were having money problems, and my mom decided that I would have to go live in a monastery in Phnom Penh. When parents couldn't take care of their kids, they brought them to the Buddhist temple. This still happens all over Cambodia.

So, when I was fourteen years old, my mom brought me to the pagoda in Phnom Penh, and left me with the monks. Sarith came to the monastery too. My brother Oum Suntoum was already there. This was June 1959.

It was the Ounalom Temple, close to the Royal Palace. In the temple there were fifty units. My unit was #43. I just went to normal school, and we also took classes about Buddhism at the temple on Wednesdays and Saturdays, but they didn't try to turn us into monks.

It was the first time I had left home and the first time I came to Phnom Penh. I missed my mother and my siblings; it was just me and my brother. But life was good at the monastery — the monks treated us well and we had plenty to eat.

My mother gave me enough money to buy a bicycle and I would ride to school and back to the temple every day, and that is when I saw Pradal Serey for the first time.

3

— Pradal Serey —

Tell me about the first time you saw Pradal Serey.

The middle school I went to was called Chamroeun Vichea. We studied French, Khmer, math and physics. I was happy being a student and always got good grades.

After school, my friends and I would ride home. Even though the pagoda was only fifteen minutes away, sometimes my friends and I would ride all over the city for hours, just for fun. One day after school, I rode through the Boeung Keng Kang district. Across the street, I saw a strange scene that fascinated me. I stopped my bike and just stared.

There were about ten men, all adults, standing around mirrors and punching the air and making funny faces. I remember thinking that they looked like monkeys. There were also big bags hanging from a tree that they were kicking.

Finally, I asked "What are they doing?" And somebody told me, "They are practicing Pradal Serey."

I walked closer to take a peek, and I had a good feeling about it. I thought to myself, "They look so stupid. I could kick the shit out of them." But I didn't know anything about fighting. I just thought I could beat anyone. I was barely five feet tall, but that made no difference to me.

The next day, I went back to the same place and begged them to let me in. The instructor said, "What are you doing here?" I said, "I am asking to be taught as a boxer." I told him I was fourteen years old and in the sixth grade. He said, "You are too small. Don't even think of it." I told him I could beat anyone. He said, "Are you crazy? Go home."

A couple days later, I went to beg him again. He said, "You come again?" He pointed at the street and told me to disappear.

Before, when I was at school, I used to always pay attention and was a very good student. But when I saw kickboxing, my brain kept thinking about being a boxer. I would spend all day in school and only think about kickboxing.

I went a third time, and they said "You — again? Okay, you can train."

I didn't own anything, except my clothes and bike. They had gloves, wrappers for their hands, mouth pieces. But I didn't have anything. They told me to go find hand-wraps. The monks had a special cloth, and while it was drying in the sun, I took a pair of scissors and cut off a piece of their cloth to wrap my hands with. And I cut out the back part of a sandal, and it perfectly fit as a mouth guard — nobody told me to do that, I just figured it out.

The instructor lived in the back house, and the school was his front house. They opened at five p.m. and I got out of school at three p.m., so I would get there an hour early and already have my hands wrapped.

There was a man named Chhay Rin. He was twenty years old and the local champion. I went to him and asked, "Can I fight with you?" He said, "What? You've only been here a few days. I'll kill you."

I told him I could beat him, and then I told the instructor I could beat him. So, they said, "Okay, you can fight," but they told him not to hurt me too bad, just teach me a lesson.

I got in the ring, and they gave me a pair of boxing gloves. They put the gloves on my hands for the first time, and I was so happy. Chhay Rin and I got in the ring, and he let me hit him. And I hit him as hard as I could because I wanted to beat him. But he got angry and decided to fight back and really let me have it. I got a bloody nose. and he bruised up my face. Both eyes and my lips were swollen.

I rode my bike back to the temple and tried to go straight to bed, but my brother and the monks saw me and asked me why my face was all beat up. I lied and told them I got in a fight at school.

The next day, I asked the instructor to quit. He said "Okay, you can quit."

How long did you stop for?

I quit for three months. But every day, no matter where I was, I was always thinking about kickboxing, so I joined another school called Reach Mondul Keila Khmer that belonged to the Royal Family. It was right next to where they take care of elephants for the king.

I went there to ask, and they didn't tell me I was too small. That's when I began to realize there were so many different types and styles of gyms in Cambodia.

There were two Pradal Serey instructors — Sok Ren and In Samm. They never asked my name. They just said go ahead and learn. Nobody taught me, I just found a corner and practiced myself. I never missed a day, and just like before, they opened at five p.m. and I was there by four p.m., with my hands wrapped. I would just keep an eye on the instructor and watch how he did certain moves, give an upper punch and stuff like that. Nobody acknowledged me, but I just kept practicing.

Three months went by like this, and then one day they said, "Hey, little guy, come here. What's your name?"

"I am Oum Ry," I said. And that day they began to teach me the theory and practice of Pradal Serey.

When In Samm saw me, he sensed I was a good fighter. He told me, "You can tell by the skin of a chicken if it is for fighting or for eating." He told me I had the natural talent to be a great fighter, if I continued to train hard.

They taught me the fundamentals — jabbing, kicking, moving your feet, moving your head. They taught me to kick with my shin and not my feet, and had me practice by kicking a banana tree for an hour a day. And they also had me train to take punches better. They would make me stand in front of a heavy bag, with my nose barely touching it. Then they would pull the bag back and let it swing right into my face so it hit me straight on the nose. I had to just stand there as they would do this over and over, so it made my nose numb and it conditioned my face to take direct hits easier.

They also told me about the strategy. For instance, I learned there are three styles of kickboxing — Close, Middle and Far. You must have skill in all three. Far is when you really extend your limbs, giving straight punches, push kicks, and sidekicks. Middle is the long knee or hooks. And the close game involves elbows and knees and clinching. Clinching is when you hold onto the back of your opponent's neck, and don't let go, so you can knee them in the ribs as much as possible.

What were you naturally best at?

My strongest skill was the close game. Second is my middle game. I don't do much of the far game because I never kicked high. I only kick ribs and legs. If my opponent and I are the same height then I can kick high, but usually I fought people who were taller than me and had more reach, so I had to get in close to do the most damage.

A few months later, In Saam said, "You are going to become a champion." I asked, "How do you know?" He said, "You go practice and you will learn, you will discover yourself, who you are."

Soon after that he told me, "You aren't going to stay at the temple anymore. You will stay at my house with my family." I told him I wanted to go to school, and he said, "That's fine. You can practice before and after." So, when I was fifteen years old, I left the temple and I moved in with Inn Som's family.

How did living with your teacher affect you?

My training intensified. I started training twice a day. I would wake up at four a.m. and train for two hours, then ride my bike back home and shower and then ride to school. Then after school, I would train from five until eight p.m. I also got to meet a lot of fighters through Inn Som and began to see the life of a professional fighter up close — and I wanted that life.

Then when I was sixteen, three important things happened in my life — I won my first professional fight, I moved out on my own, and I discovered the exciting world of beautiful women.

My first paid fight was in Kampong Cham Province — I made three hundred riel in that fight, and gave half of it to my teacher. The guy who I fought against was named Sinkin.

I was sixteen and he was thirty-six years old. I had trained for two years already. I got hit so many times that by the third round my face was so swollen that my eyes started to shut. My coach then threw in the towel, but I ran and grabbed it and threw it back at him and yelled that I wanted to keep fighting.

By the fourth round, my face was completely covered in blood, and my teacher threw in the towel again, and this time jumped into the ring and grabbed me from behind so I couldn't fight anymore.

I tried quitting again and even moved back to the temple in Phnom Penh to live with the monks. But Inn Som came to the temple to ask me to come back and continue fighting.

My next fight was a couple months later, and it ended in a draw. But I was learning what I needed to become a winner. After the draw, I asked my teacher what I was doing right and wrong. He just said, "Your knees are excellent, focus on your knees," so I started training even harder.

My first professional win was in the province of Kampong Cham against a guy named Pbork Van Soueng. He was taller and wider than me. There were about two thousand people in the audience, and we were one of the early fights. For the first two rounds it was pretty even, but then in the third round, all of a sudden, I started attacking with my knees. I locked and clinched his neck and kneed him in the face so many times that when I let go of his neck he just dropped to the ground. It was my first win and my first knock out. I was overwhelmed with joy. My teacher came to me after the fight and said, "You will be the champion one day."

So, your first fight was a loss, your second was a draw, and your third was a win?

Yes. That is how it happened. And from that third fight on, I just kept winning. Between 1963 and 1967, I fought around fifty times. At least once a month, sometimes more. I won almost every fight — I only lost a few times and it was always on points — I never got knocked out. And I was slowly building a name for myself. And people really liked me because I was so much smaller than my opponents, but I would chase them around like a cat chasing a mouse.

While I was in school, I got a job as a security guard at a bus station. I saved some money and with Sarith rented a house in the Khan Russey neighborhood, right in front of a whorehouse. The walls and the roof were built of palm leaves, and there was just one open room where about six of us lived. There wasn't enough space for everyone to sleep, so we turned the mattress horizontally, having everyone sleep with their feet dangling off.

And it was just a matter of time until I discovered the clubs. In Cambodia those days, there weren't rules about age restrictions. You could box at ten years old and get beat up and it was normal — there was no amateur class, you just started fighting as a professional. It's not about your age, it's about how mature you are. I was a teenager, but I spent a lot of time training with men who were older than me and I lived alone, so I was very mature.

I loved being in the club — I drank soda because it was cheap, and I was a very good singer. But I was mostly interested in all the women I could meet.

I have very fond memories of the woman who first taught me about sex. Her name was Yann, and she was a very beautiful Chinese Cambodian with white skin from the province of Kampot. She was twenty-one, and I was sixteen. She was the manager at the Kang Sann Club, and one night she told me she didn't have a husband and invited me to her house. When we got to her place, I sat on her bed, and I was so nervous because I didn't know what to do with her. She asked me if I loved her, and I said, "Yes, I love you like a sister." And she said, "No, tonight we are going to love each other like husband and wife." She began to slowly take off her clothes and show me her body, and then she gave me my first taste. I was young and very energetic, and neither of us slept that night.

We saw each other for a bit after that, but I started seeing other girls at different clubs too. Back in those days, my neck was big and muscular and almost the same size as my head. And I had a beautiful nose back then. But now my nose has been broken so many times that it is flat because it has no bone left.

4.

◆ Champion ◆

When did you become a champion?

I became a champion when I was eighteen years old. The French cognac company Martel had a tournament with six-teen fighters, and all the news media was there. To win the trophy, a fighter had to win four fights in one night.

The first person I fought with was Prum Serey, a famous fighter from Battambang, and I knocked him out in the first half of the first round by kneeing him in his ribs and stomach. In the second match, I fought Tiv Sok who I beat by decision. And then I went to the semi-final. There I met the teacher Tchea Tung. I knocked him out in the third round with my knee and my elbow. It was between me and Chuey Bam Ol for the main event. I kicked him and he slipped through the ropes and fell out of the ring, but he crawled back in. Then I knocked him out in the fifth round, with the knee and elbow again.

People were amazed because I was so small, I was only five-foot-six and one hundred thirty-five pounds, and all my opponents were much bigger. But I had a lot of heart, and the audience could feel it. I became famous even though I was still in school.

The next month, I had to take a test for my diploma. If I passed, I could go to the government's school for free, but if I failed, I would have to pay for private school. But all my thoughts were about how to fight better, and I didn't pay too much attention at school, so I failed my exam. My family didn't know I was fighting, but when I became a champion, they heard it announced on the radio. And my mother was so upset, she decided she didn't want to see or talk to me anymore.

I went to visit her in Kampong Luong with many gifts and money, and she shut the door in my face and refused to let me in. She said, "I work hard so that you can go to school to become a teacher, not to become a fighter." She had an idea of the type of people boxers were, and she hated it. All my siblings were either instructors or studying to become instructors — there was nobody like a boxer in my family.

I begged her, "Please, Mom! I have money and gifts for you." She yelled from the other side of the front door, "I don't want your blood money! What do you think you will get from fighting? You can't make a career from boxing. You can only get hurt or die!"

I didn't know how to answer. I wanted her to know that I studied at the same time that I trained and never missed school. All I could say was, "But, Mom, I am famous."

"I don't care how famous you are," she yelled at me. "You are making me suffer!" I promised her I would continue in school and get my degree, even if I had to pay for it. All I could do was leave the gifts by her front door and go back home to the city.

You failed school because you thought about fighting too much, but then you had to fight in order to pay for the private school?

Yes, three hundred riel for three months. I didn't want my mom to feel bad that I wasn't in school. I was determined to do both.

During the school year, I would train twice a day, but on holidays and the summer, I would train three times a day — I would wake up at four a.m. and run ten kilometers. Then I rested and trained from eight to ten a.m. I kicked the bag, shadowboxed, lifted weights and did one thousand push-ups a day — two hundred at a time, five times a day. Night training was from five to eight p.m. I'd jump rope for one hour straight. It's very good for your body because it keeps you light, like you're flying. I only rested on Sundays.

And on Sundays, I would go see movies. In 1963, I saw a Bruce Lee film called *The Thunderstorm*. I couldn't stop thinking about his style and his moves. After the movie, I didn't want to talk. My friend who came with me asked me, "Are you upset? What happened?" I said, "I am thinking about fighting." I figured out how to incorporate some of his ideas into Pradal Serey. I was inspired by how stealthy and fast he was. Bruce Lee is very tiny but mighty.

But my favorite was Clint Eastwood. Back then, you could buy one ticket and stay in the movie theater all day. I would watch *The Good, The Bad and The Ugly* over and over. I was very inspired by him. The way he would draw his gun so quickly and win the battle. I watched, and I decided to fight like that. To just go straight in, fast, hard, and be the quickest draw. In fact, many times before a fight I would think about my grandmother and Clint Eastwood. These two people inspired my fighting style more than anybody else.

My most powerful move was to clinch the neck and knee them in the ribs. Many fighters could clinch the neck and use their knees, but they could only do it a few times before they would get tired, or the fighters would break away from each other. I could hold on and kick fast and hard, over and over. A spectator told me once, "Your knee is fast and hard like a machine, like the pistons of an engine." They nicknamed me "Chun Kung Yunn," which translates to "Machine Knee." I practiced my knees two hours a day.

I wasn't scared of anyone. I literally thought, "Why does anyone dare fight me?" That's why I always won, because even though I was small for a fighter, I saw everyone as smaller than me.

But also, I was a gentleman. I did not do any bragging, if I knocked people down, I would help them get up. Some fighters don't care. If someone falls, they kick them more. And when I won, I would never jump on top of the ropes and show off. And I would always thank the audience for supporting the sport — I always bowed my head down and respected the people around me.

This was my conscience. I always remember my grandmother saying to me, "Be calm, be kind, be brave."

When did you become the national champion?

I became the national champion in 1967. I fought against Chea Sarak. He came from Siem Reap Province. He was a big, strong man with very long legs and kicked faster than anyone, so he was excellent with the far fighting style. We were the two best fighters in Cambodia, and outside the ring we became good friends. Though our personalities were very different — he was loud and an arrogant show-off, he would break tables at restaurants, and if he all of a sudden felt like singing, he would just go and grab the microphone right out of the singer's hands. I was the opposite. I respected everyone, and all the club owners would give me food and drinks because they knew I was a kind person.

Tell me about the fight.

It was set up by Chai Chaing, who was the biggest promoter at the time. He asked me if I wanted to fight Chea Sarak for the championship, and I said, "Of course." I never said no to a fight. But Chea Sarak was at least three inches taller than me, and at least twenty pounds heavier, so he was in a higher weight class. Chai Chaing told me I needed to gain weight to qualify. I began to eat a lot more, especially a lot of rice. But I didn't gain so much weight. When it was time for the weigh in, I put some heavy metal balls in my underwear which helped me get into the higher weight class.

We fought at the Olympic Stadium, and it was standing room only. The energy was electric in the stadium that night, because everyone knew they were watching the two best Pradal Serey fighters in all of Cambodia fight for the first time.

The first round, I was just feeling him out, not overdoing it, doing a lot of defense — he would kick me, and I dodged all his kicks. But I was studying him the whole time. Some fighters switch their style every round, some just have the same style all the time. I could tell that Chea Sarak always fought with the same style.

Since Chea Sarak was from the country, and I was a Phnom Penh city boy, the crowd was with me that night. In the second round, I came out more aggressive with my close game, and the audience could feel the heat. When he would kick me, for just a moment he would be exposed, so I would go inside fast for an attack. It was an even fight in the third round, but in the fourth I clinched him and used my knees on his side, at least ten fast and hard knees to his ribs before he broke free. In the fifth round, I knocked him down, again with my knees, but he got up on the eight count. Because there was no knock-out, it went to the judges to decide. Chea Sarak won the first round 10-9, second round was 9-9, third and fourth rounds I won 9-10, and because I knocked him down in the fifth round, I won that 8-10. Overall, I won 50-47.

The audience exploded in applause. It was one of the most beautiful moments in my life to feel the entire stadium screaming my name and cheering. When the announcer gave the microphone to Chea Sarak, he instantly said, "I want a rematch." When they gave the mic to me, all I said was, "Of course. I'm ready for you anytime."

We would wind up fighting six times over the next three years — two wins, two losses, and two draws.

At that time, I had many fights at the Olympic Stadium — we fought there once a month. But we also went out to the provinces to fight. Sometimes I fought three times in a month. Cambodia has twenty-four provinces, and I fought in each. Nobody beat me. And before the fights, when I would enter the stadium and head to the ring, women would scream my name and wave the towels, and it'd give me more energy and power to fight.

Did you have any serious injuries?

Yes, from one of the times I fought against Chea Sarak — he broke my sternum. He kicked me hard, and I fell back, and he fell on my chest with his knee. I could hear the crunch. I stayed until the fifth round and lost from points. I went home and went to sleep, and the next day I couldn't get up. My girlfriend had to wheel me to the hospital in her cyclo.*

---

* A common sight in Cambodia and Southeast Asia, a cyclo has a seat on the front, is pedaled like a bicycle but has three wheels. It is commonly used as a taxi.

I had to take three months off to recover. And of course, no one will pay for you, you have to pay for yourself.

What about long-term injuries?

I can't hear out of my left ear — I got hit in the ear so many times. And I don't have any teeth left. They got knocked out from people's knees. And, like I said, my nose is totally flat because the bone has been broken so many times. And my shoulders hurt because they have been dislocated so often. But fortunately, I still have an excellent memory and can think clearly. And I still run two to four miles on the beach every day.

Did you have a ritual before every fight?

Yes, I did a traditional dance called the Twai Kru. Everyone does their own dance and has their own style. Mine is short and sweet. But it is a moment to pay respect to your teachers and elders. And, of course, to my guardian spirit Ta Kaan. One hundred percent of the Cambodian and Thai boxers believe in a guardian spirit. Everyone believes in different spirits, but you must believe in something.

The Twai Kru also helps you focus. I was very good at keeping focus. What people don't realize about focus is that we must learn to manage our own mind. You must know yourself, and who you are, and what is important to you. If you can learn to do that, you can turn a fire into a laser. When I would get in the ring, I never thought about anything else but fighting and winning. I didn't think about women or money or anything else — there is plenty of time for that later.

After the fight, we all went to the club, even if we were just trying to beat the shit out of each other in the ring. We were all friends. Every night was a different club — Sovann

Macha, Reatrey Sour, Mekong Club, and La Lune... Usually our faces were beat up and bruised from the fight, but we would just wear sunglasses and sing. I love singing.

Tell me more about the clubs, what they were like.

There were two types, dancing clubs and night clubs, which were more like bars or restaurants. At each club, there would be twenty or thirty young women who were called "hostesses." When you sat at your table, you could choose any girl you want, and she would come over to your table and sit and talk with you, keep you company, or dance. The man would buy a drink — the most popular drinks then were French cognac and Cambodian beer — and say the drink was ten riel, the woman would get seven and the bar owner would get three. Then it all depended on how the man and woman got along. If they had a good conversation and liked each other, sometimes the man would pay her for sex, or if she really liked him, she would do it for free because she wanted to.

In those years, life was very good. Between 1965 to 1970 was an amazing time to be in Cambodia — we had peace, and young people were getting influenced by the western music and styles. It was a very creative time. Because Pradal Serey was the national sport, and I was the national champion, I became friends with the most famous people in Cambodia. Sinn Sisamouth was the most popular singer in Cambodia and was a big boxing fan and always had so many questions for me. The top movie star was Kong Som Eun, and he and I became very close friends.[4]

At the time, there was only one bank in Cambodia, so I kept all my money in my pocket, at all times. It was very easy for me to spend, spend, spend. And because I was handsome and famous and had money, many women wanted to be with me. Very beautiful women, too many to count.

Wasn't it difficult being with women and having sex when your body gets so beat up?

It wasn't so hard. I healed quickly.

When was your first serious relationship?

That was in 1964 with Khou Kimny — we met at the market, and she was the first woman I got pregnant. But I met another girl the next month named Khun Own — she was half Khmer and half Vietnamese — and because she sold peanuts at the stadium, she would watch me fight all the time, and I got her pregnant also.

The two kids were born three months apart. Khou Kimny's child was a boy named Oum Vuthy, and Khun Own's baby was named Oum Chantrea. The next year, I had another child with Khou Kimny, and we named him Oum Pee. This is your brother who I have been talking to on Facebook.

I didn't live with either woman because I was busy training all the time. Nobody trained harder than me. Back then, I dropped kids everywhere, I was very careless about that. I do have regrets — I was not a good father, and I didn't take care of my kids like I should have.

But it was important that I keep these two women away from each other because they would fight every time they met. Every time. Sarith was my towel and water boy at the fights, and one night had to break them up — they both came to watch me at the stadium, and they got into a brawl, at the fight! They handed their babies to other people while they punched each other. Both wound up getting arrested, and I had to go to the jail to get them out. Fortunately, the police were boxing fans and they helped me. But people teased me for so long for being the fighter with the two fighting wives.

Did you miss being part of your family? Did your mother and family accept you back into their lives?

Eventually, I reconnected with my family, and they accepted me again. But my mother didn't let me forget that she didn't like fighters and that I hurt her by not becoming a teacher like my siblings.

When did things start getting politically tense?

It began in 1970, when King Sihanouk was thrown out of power. Some say the King was bad, some said the king was good. Different opinions. I wasn't into politics that much, I just thought about training. That is when I first heard the name Khmer Rouge, but they were far out in the country, and they hadn't attacked the city yet. People didn't think too much about them.

When King Sihanouk was out of the country on a trip, the military seized control, and a general named Lon Nol took over the government. This was the first time in Cambodian history that we did not have a king. It was a big shock for the older generations, but the younger people wanted a change.

Also, the Viet Kong were invading Cambodia in the northeast because they were trying to smuggle weapons from the North to the South through the Ho Chi Minh Trail in their fight against the Americans. In 1970, the Americans started bombing the Cambodian side of the Vietnam border, but at the same time they destroyed entire villages and killed many innocent Cambodian people.[5] This attracted the country people to join the Khmer Rouge because they promised to support the people against the foreigners. It also caused refugees to leave the country and come to the city to look for work. From 1970 to 1975, the population of Phnom Penh went from five hundred thousand to two million — in just five years. There was so much traffic, and people were building houses everywhere you looked.

Then in April 1970, the new American-backed government of Lon Nol decided to shut down much of the cultural life of the country in an attempt to reorganize. They shut down the sport program — there was to be no sports or entertainment. And all men were encouraged to join the army to help defend the country. Since I couldn't fight to earn money for a while, I went into the army in 1970. Almost every athlete wound up going into the army.

Lon Nol takes over, shuts down all the sports in the country and you went to possibly fight a war? Were you upset that your life changed so suddenly?

I wasn't angry. Actually, I was happy, because I was defending my country from being invaded by the Vietnamese.

But I was only on the front line for a short time. After a week we came back down to the base, and the commander of the camp heard that I was a soldier and ordered me to go see him. He said, "Do you want to be on the front line or be my bodyguard?" I said, "I want to stay with you." He gave me an M-16 and a pistol to protect him. Wherever the commander went, I went with him.

I was a bodyguard for almost an entire year when we got word that the government decided to restart the sports program because the people needed entertainment. Sports were important for people to bond and feel good, and I think they could tell people were getting restless without entertainment to watch. In December 1971, the government sent a helicopter to pick me up and take me back to Phnom Penh in order for me to start training again.

The government created a community for all the athletes to live at and work at. It was called Borei Keila, and there were apartments, dining halls and training facilities. And there were all sorts of sports there — swimming, basketball, soccer, wrestling, and of course, Pradal Serey.

This was great because I was back to training twice a day, three times if I had a fight coming, and I was still getting my army salary, plus money from fights. And all the athletes lived in the sports facility, so our rent and food were paid for.

Then in July of 1972, I fought for the International Championship against a Thai champ named Midet Nay in Phnom Penh. It was held at the Faculty of Science, in a giant outdoor space. There were about ten thousand people in the audience, and there were ten fights, with me against the Thai as the main event.

This was the first time that the Thai fighters had come to Cambodia since our governments decided to restart relations. Back in 1963, the kings of Cambodia and Thailand got in a feud over the ancient temple Preah Vihear, which is right on the border of both countries.[6] The borders were closed, and all cultural exchange stopped. This lasted all the way until 1970, when the international court ruled in favor of Cambodia. For nine years, there were no fights between Pradal Serey and Muay Thai fighters.

Midet Nay was an excellent fighter. He was tall, with long legs and long arms, so he could fight from a distance and keep me from getting too close to him where I could do some damage. The first two rounds, I was just trying to figure out his style and how I could make an opening. He had a really good defense and I couldn't get close to him. Then in the third round, he knocked me down with a punch to my face. I fell down, and the judge started counting me out. I was down for eight counts but got back up in time.

Then five seconds after I got on my feet, the bell rang. I could go back to my corner and try to catch my breath.

Entering round four, I realized I had to change my thinking and strategy — I had to bring the fight close to him. I was good with counterattack and realized when he would lift his legs to kick me, that was my opportunity for close contact. Like

I saw from the Clint Eastwood movies, I just went straight in as quickly as possible. I was able to find an opening and clinched his neck and started kneeing him in the front and sides of his stomach. I cliched him for so long that I was able to drag him all around the ring and knee him forty times. I know this because the audience started counting every time I kneed him — *Muoy! Pir! Bei! Buon!* Back then, my knees were so fast, like lightning, and I could use them from many directions. Then I got some good elbows into his face.

I had hurt his stomach so much that in the middle of round five, he started throwing up all over the ring and couldn't stop vomiting. The referee stopped the fight. All the judges pushed their chairs back to avoid getting sprayed, and I was declared the winner.

At this point, I got even more famous because not only was I the international champion, but now there were color TVs in many clubs and restaurants. People now knew what I looked like, because in the 1960s it was only on the radio.

Did you ever fight outside of Cambodia?

I fought in Vietnam in 1970, and in both Malaysia and Burma in 1972. But they were very easy fights, and I knocked them out. Everyone knew that the best fighters were in Cambodia and Thailand.

What is the difference between Pradal Serey and Muay Thai?

They are the same thing — mostly the same rules and same styles. But in Cambodia, you can clinch them longer. When you're clinching and hit the rope, they tell you to stop. In Cambodia, the final decision is made by the judge. In Thailand, it depends on the referee.

What was your experience fighting later in Thailand?

A cop who spoke both Khmer and Thai organized a trip for Cambodian and Thai New Years, April 13, 1973. He arranged for six fighters from Cambodia to fight all around Thailand for three weeks. We drove for two days and then took a ten-hour boat ride. When we finally got there, we had two days to rest and then we started the fighting. We were paid one thousand baht, which was about forty dollars.

My first fight was with a Malaysian, but I finished him off easily. Because I barely sustained any damage, I was able to fight again the next day.

The next fight was with a Thai, and we went five rounds. He was good with his legs and kicked way more than me. For the first and second rounds, I couldn't figure out his style. I had to test him and observe, and in the third round I was finally able to get a read and predict his moves. He kicked me with his right leg, so I moved to the right and clinched him then kneed and elbowed him. I knocked him down three times, and I never fell — that's why I won by decision.

The Thai audience obviously sided with their own people and since I was the new guy, no one cheered for me. When the Thais would win, it would get very loud, and they would play music and cheer. As soon as I beat him, it was so quiet in the stadium, you could almost hear crickets.

We usually got five days to rest between fights, so I had some time off to explore Thailand. The other fighters were stingy and didn't want to spend money. I like to enjoy myself and have fun, so I hired a twelve-year-old boy to be a translator; I paid him twenty baht (one dollar) per day. If I wanted to connect with a girl, I told him to translate, "Honey, I love you" in Thai.

I was impressed that Thai women didn't wear dresses but bell bottoms. They caught on to fashion trends quicker. Cambodians didn't adopt the Western style like Thais did.

But a few years later, the Cambodian women eventually caught up.

Also, when I was in Thailand, I heard "Black Magic Woman" by Santana for the first time and fell in love with his music, and I still love it.

For our third set of fights, we had to drive for six hours to get to the town of Trat. I fought Ratana Visalsak. Just like I had done in my last fight, for the first and second rounds, we felt each other out, but in the third round he was difficult for me to grab. He kicked and moved very quickly — I've never dealt with a fighter who I couldn't clinch. It ended up being a draw. Even though I feel I should have won on points, he was a champion of the Trat province, and I think they didn't want to embarrass him in front of his Thai fans.

In the last fight, they matched me with a Thai guy who lied and said he wasn't a champion, but he was. His name was Virak Chhay. He had very good defense. Every time I kicked him in the rib cage, he'd grab my leg under my knee and sweep me with his opposite leg. The third round, I thought maybe I had no hope. I still had pain from the previous fight. As soon as I clinched him, he was so strong he was able to push me out. He won by one point.

The police guy who organized the whole trip told me not to go back to Cambodia because if I stayed in Thailand, I'd make a lot of money. But I missed Cambodia, and I missed all my girlfriends too much.

How many professional fights did you have in your career?

I fought continuously from 1960 to 1975, except for the one year between 1970 and 1971, when they shut down the entire sports program. For those fifteen years, I fought about three hundred fights. I won them all except I lost maybe thirty by decision, and had three draws. And I was never knocked out.

I was unique because I had a very long career of winning. Some fighters get famous for only a year or two before they burn out. Since I dislocated my shoulder at least five times by 1974, I started to lose more. But I never thought of retiring. If I was asked to fight, I would always say yes.

Those years, 1972 to 1974, were the best years of my life. I had total freedom. And everywhere I went, people treated me like a superstar. All the women loved to be seen with the famous boxer. I could pick any woman I wanted.

With all your girlfriends, did you ever fall in love with any of them?

In the spring of 1974, I met a woman named Pich Dovann and our lives would become very intertwined. It was very random how we met. I was riding on a motorcycle and she and her friend were on a bicycle after getting out of school. I saw her on the back of the bike and was enchanted by her beauty, she had a body like a model. I rode up next to her to say hello and she started cussing at me, saying I was annoying and to leave her alone. I followed her until she got home and stood outside her apartment building. She went up to the third floor and looked out the window and saw me — she spat at me. But I knew that she liked me, or she wouldn't have looked out the window.

The next day I went back and stood outside her building until she came out. "You again?" she yelled. But I was persistent, and she reluctantly agreed to go have lunch with me at the Central Market. We fell in love, and a month later she was pregnant with my child.

In your life, you were thriving, but at the same time the political situation was deteriorating?

Yes. The Khmer Rouge had grown in numbers and strength.

And they were being armed by the Chinese communists and were determined to destabilize the society in order to get rid of the Lon Nol government and get rid of all the foreigners. They wanted to take Cambodia back to its original greatness, which they referred to as Angkar. They organized a guerrilla war against the innocent people in Phnom Penh by throwing grenades in movie theaters and restaurants to make people not want to go out. They even shot rockets into the city at night, sometimes for two hours at a time, which would land randomly and cause much damage and fear. Their plan was to destroy the functioning of daily life.

Things were getting worse and worse, but nobody had any idea how truly horrible it would become.

In February 1975, Pich Dovann gave birth to our baby girl, just two months before the Khmer Rouge entered Phnom Penh.

5

— Genocide —

Did you ever think that the Khmer Rouge could actually take over the entire country one day?

I never thought we'd lose the war because we had the Americans behind us.

But then in 1975, when the Americans pulled out of Vietnam, they took all their forces out of all of Southeast Asia, including Cambodia, and the Lon Nol government quickly collapsed.

It all happened so fast. The next day, the Khmer Rouge entered Phnom Penh in tanks.

It was April 17th. People were celebrating because they thought we finally had peace. We thought they wanted to put Cambodia back together as one.

What were you doing that morning?

I was at home. I was living with Pich Dovann and our new two-month-old baby. I went outside to see what was happening — tanks were rolling down the city streets, with men in black clothing sitting on top. Then I heard gunshots. I went back inside and grabbed all my army clothes and threw them in the trash. I knew enough about communists from being in the army to know that communists will never allow peace to exist. I knew this was very bad news.

I thought about my children and my mom and my family everywhere. I didn't know how to connect with anyone because there were no telephones back then and they had blocked all the roads going in and out of the city. There was no way to go find them.

Then the next day, the Khmer Rouge told everyone to evacuate the city. We had one day to pack everything and move out. They lied to us and said the Americans are going to bomb the entire city, so you must get out.

We couldn't take anything — no pictures, no clothes, nothing. People just grabbed whatever jewelry they had and whatever food they could carry with them. We were lucky to find Pich Dovann's mother, sister and entire family. We were a group of ten total. We just started walking out of the city. I pushed an ox cart with all the food we brought with us, and Pich Dovann carried the baby in her arms.

How many people were on the road?

It seemed like hundreds of thousands. There were about two million people who lived in Phnom Penh, so it was a sea of humans filling the roads. If someone disobeyed orders, they'd get shot. I saw people standing close to me getting shot. I was very scared. I began to hear that they were killing anybody who worked for the government, was a teacher, or people who spoke a foreign language, or who were famous.

And Pich Dovann's family were of Vietnamese descent, so if the Khmer Rouge found out, they would be executed. I began to really worry, but there was nothing we could do, except keep going forward.

Were strangers helping each other?

Sometimes, but everyone mostly thought about staying alive, so no one could really help each other.

At night, people would just fall asleep on the side of the road, in the dirt, or if you were lucky, under a tree. And the only food people had to eat was just what they had brought with them.

The ten of us walked for seventeen days, until we got to a town called Tram Khnar. When we got there, we were told we were all going to be farmers. I had never been on a farm in my life — I didn't even know what a cow looked like, but now I was going to be a farmer.

At first, we all slept on the ground, but soon we were able to gather some bamboo and build a small shelter.

Within two months, our baby daughter got malaria and became very sick, very quickly. There was nothing we could do to help her because there was no medicine, and there was barely any food. She died after two weeks. I had to bury her not far from where we were sleeping. Pich Dovann was screaming and crying like nothing I had ever heard, but I could not allow myself to feel sadness. I told her she must stop crying or they would kill us. You were not even allowed to cry for your own child's death.

And we began to experience a level of brutality that nobody ever imagined. The Khmer Rouge had a saying they would often tell people before killing them, "To destroy you is no loss, to preserve you is no gain." It is well known that they killed many babies by grabbing their legs so to whip their heads against a big tree to save bullets.

At the same time, they told us that all Cambodians are now equal, except, of course, for the Khmer Rouge because they had all the weapons and power. And the entire population was divided into two groups — the new people and the old people. The new people were those from the city, like me and my family. The old people were the farmers in the country, and they had more privileges than we had, like they could cook food for themselves in their own homes, whereas we had to go to the mess hall to be served watery rice porridge, with very little rice.

What were the Khmer Rouge soldiers like?

They all wore black uniforms with a black cap and a red scarf. At the beginning, there were some that were nice to people. But if they were too nice to us, they would be executed. From the very top, the soldiers were trained and encouraged to be heartless and cruel. And since the Khmer Rouge was made up of country people, none were educated. They believed what they were told without asking questions. They were brainwashed. They were told that for the revolution to succeed, there must be no forgiving.

There were a lot of child soldiers too, and they could be very dangerous because that was the only life they knew. Some were so young that their rifle was almost bigger than they were. One time I saw a child soldier, twelve or thirteen, tell a man to get on his knees so it would be easier for him to kick him in the head.

But we never really knew who they were or why this was happening. We were just told that the revolution was to get rid of all the Yoan, or the foreigners, and the Western imperialists, who had corrupted our society with vanity and greed.

Then in the beginning of 1976, they told us we were going to move and live somewhere else. They put thousands of people on a train, and we went up to Pursat in the Pursat province. We slept one night there and then got on another train to Kat Char. I remember thousands of people getting off the train and just scrambling, looking for a place to rest.

Me and Pich Dovann's family found a small area, under a big tree and decided that's where we'd sleep. The very first evening we were there, I was cooking rice at sunset when four Khmer Rouge soldiers arrested me in front of the entire family. They said, "We know you are Oum Ry." I have no idea how they knew who I was, but they tied my arms behind my back, not at the wrists, but up by my biceps and carried me away. My family thought, the second they tie you up, you're as good as dead, and that would be the last time they see me.

They made me walk for five hours to the Kok Trum detention center. When I got there, I realized it was a prison for famous people and people who worked for the government.

I stayed there for a month. We had to work all day long, digging trenches. At night, a hundred men slept on the wooden floor, and every single night the Khmer Rouge would come in and pull out two or three to kill. I think it was totally random who they picked. Every night I would think, "Tonight they may bring me to be killed." I was barely able to sleep.

The Khmer Rouge leader of the prison was named Yen Boun. When he found out that I was in the detention center, he summoned me to go see him. Again, I thought, this must be it. I am going to die today.

When I was brought to him, Yen Boun said to me, "I am a fighter too." I remembered his name, but he wasn't a very good or famous fighter. He asked me, "Oum Ry, do you have a family?" I said, "Yes, sir. My daughter died, but I have a family." He asked me, "Do you miss your family? You want to go see them?" I said, "Yes, sir."

Then Yen Boun found out where my Pich Dovann and her family had moved since I was arrested, and gave me some rice and dried fish and a letter signed by him in case I was stopped by more Khmer Rouge soldiers. "You are a fighter like me," he told me. "Go see your family."

He told me Pich Dovann and her family moved to Khtum Prahong, and I set out by foot to find them. I had never been to this part of Cambodia, so everywhere I went, I had to ask directions. I walked for seven days, but I found them.

Pich Dovann couldn't believe it when she first saw me because ninety-nine percent of the time when they take you away, you are dead. She said she felt like she was reborn when she saw me. We hugged each other and cried.

We lived in Khtum Prahong for about six months. During these years, some people were lucky if they stayed in a region where they had food, but most were unlucky. Khtum Prahong was a relatively new town so there were no farms in the area close by, so there was no food. When I got there, there were about five hundred families, and by time we were told to leave, there were only one hundred families left. Everyone else starved. I saw several assassinations in those years. But seeing that type of thing was rare, most of the killing was done out of sight. Mostly I would see people dying from starvation or diarrhea.

One day, I went to go check in on our neighbor, a woman named Path. They had killed her husband, and soon after, she had given birth to her first child, a baby girl. When I went into her hut, she told me the baby had died, from malaria, the same thing that killed my daughter. But she said she was so hungry, that she had cooked her baby into a soup and was eating her to stay alive. She offered me some, but I said no, and told her, "If they find out what you are doing, they will kill you." Then she pleaded "No, brother, please don't tell them. I am so hungry." Three days later, Path was dead of starvation.

At that same time, I got fortunate and got a job as a grave-digger, so my family fared better because for every corpse I buried, I would receive one extra bowl of rice. The first body I buried was the corpse of my neighbor Path, the woman who ate her baby.

There were two grave diggers, me and a former soldier for Lon Nol who had lied about his identity. We built a stretcher out of bamboo, and whenever someone died, we would go to their family and collect the body. Sometimes the families were crying, sometimes the tears had run out and people were just numb. It would take about an hour to dig a shallow grave, and we each buried four or five bodies a day in the rice fields, seven days a week. I had blisters on my hands from shoveling so much. And we had no masks, but after enough time, I didn't even think about the smell anymore. At night, the coyotes would come and dig up the graves, eat what they could and make a horrible mess. But I was getting enough food to feed my family, so I was lucky.

But at any moment, that luck could run out because we could be selected to be killed for no reason. Even if our bodies were still alive, our personalities were dying because we lost all our freedoms, and the worst is that we lost our ability to make any decisions.

Another thing that the Khmer Rouge would do, is if they decided to kill a man, they would very often kill his entire family too because they didn't want to have to deal with kids who would grow up and want revenge. They would say, "To kill a weed, you must also destroy the roots."

Around August of 1977, we were told that we were moving to a town called Phnom Arai and that I was to be a farmer again. Our life consisted of waking up at five a.m. to work in the rice fields, then at noon we got one bowl of rice porridge, with much more water than rice, and then we got an hour to rest, and would get back to farming until nighttime. The weather didn't matter — there could be a monsoon, or terrible heat, and we would have to work all day, every day. And of course, we didn't have things like toothbrushes, or soap, or even an extra pair of clothes. And nobody complained because they knew they would instantly be killed for thinking they were better than anybody else and not sacrificing for Angkar. Every Cambodian lived this way, except for those who were actually in power.

What were the skills you needed to survive?

Very simple. Learn to lie. Lie all the time. Everything was a secret, and you should trust no one. You had to live like a shadow, so nobody noticed you, so you didn't stand out. And act dumb all the time, like you knew nothing. Don't ask any questions, don't complain. But at the same time, we all had to learn to steal. If you couldn't steal, you might not eat at all. But the most important skill was just to keep thinking about surviving — every day was just an attempt to make it one more day.

For example, soon after we got to Phnom Arai, word got around to some of the Khmer Rouge that Oum Ry the fighter was there. They came to find me and brought along a blacksmith, whose name was also Ry. He was very tall, five-foot-eleven, well fed and muscular, and they wanted us to fight for their entertainment. I'm confident I could have beat him, but I also knew that if I embarrassed him, he would have me and my family killed. Win or lose, if I fought him, they would kill me. So, I lied. I said, "He's too big and too strong. Please don't make me fight him. He will break me." They laughed at me, but eventually left me alone. Sometimes you need to win with the brain, and not your fists.

Another time where I was noticed in Phnom Arai was on an afternoon when I was working with an ox inside a barn, milling rice. While working I realized that eleven Khmer Rouge soldiers were peeking at me from a hole in the wall. When I saw them, I felt like all the blood left my body, and I thought I might pass out.

The leader of this group called to me from outside and said, "I have different food — go over there and eat it." I tried to refuse and say that I had already eaten, but he said, "Don't eat that rice soup anymore. It has no taste." Instead, he gave me kor — pork and eggs in a sweet soup. I became even more convinced that they were going to kill me because I've watched movies, and they offer the prisoner a final meal before he is executed.

He then said to me, "I've only heard your name, but now I meet you in person!" He was a big Pradal Serey fan and would listen to my fights on the radio. I have no idea how he knew who I was, and I never was told his name, though he seemed to be very high ranking in the Khmer Rouge. He said to me, "We were passing by this area, and I heard you were here. I decided to come see you for myself." He asked how I became such a good fighter even though I am so small. He asked me to show him some boxing moves. Then I showed him my broken nose and told him how I can't hear from one ear, and my broken chest.

He commanded the local Khmer Rouge soldiers to always make sure I was given good food, and I always shared that food with the nine other men who worked on that farm. It had been years since any of us had eaten real food, and especially meat. We felt very lucky.

During that time, twice I randomly met people who I was very close to before the war — Chea Sarak and my older sister.

Chea Sarak was my friend but also my strongest competitor. Like I mentioned earlier, we fought six times at the Olympic Stadium — two wins, two losses and two draws. We always remained good friends, no matter how much we wanted to beat each other up.

He was coming from Bo Preah, the province near the Vietnamese border. I think he got a job as a bodyguard for one of the leaders of the Khmer Rouge and for some reason, the group he was in came through Phnom Arai and we just happened to meet coincidentally. We gave each other a hug, that's it. We didn't want anyone to see us get emotional with each other. We talked for half an hour, and he said to me, "Be careful — the Khmer Rouge are beginning to fight amongst themselves." He told me that a faction from the west accused a faction from the east of conspiring with the Vietnamese, so they were sending their soldiers this way to execute them.

At one time, Chea Sarak and I were on top of the world — we had fame, and money and women. And now we were surrounded by death, and our biggest accomplishment was just surviving another day.

Later I heard he was killed very close to the end of the war. I was told that they had taken him to be executed and he fought back. He knocked a few of them down, but they had guns, so they shot him.

The other chance encounter happened when I was transporting some food on the ox cart, and I saw someone I knew from my childhood, and he said my older sister Oum Sarom was staying in the town of Phum Chrey. She was there with her five children — her husband was a doctor and died from malaria the year before. I took a big risk in trying to find her, but when I finally rode up to her hut, we were so happy to see each other. It was the first time either of us had seen any of our family in the three years since the war started. Of course, the first thing I asked about was our mother, but she had no news.

Oum Sarom told me that she was organizing a wedding for her son Ravy for the following week, so I told her I would bring some potatoes and some fruit for the wedding. A week later I returned with one hundred kilograms of rice and potatoes. But when I got there, the Khmer Rouge was in the middle of arresting my sister.

Ravy decided he didn't want to get married, so he escaped. The Khmer Rouge said he went to join Serey Ka, the "freedom fighters," which was an armed group who fought against the Khmer Rouge.

I stopped and got off my cart and the detective asked, "What's your relation to her?" I said, "She's my sister." He told me, "High ranking people told me to arrest your sister and the rest of her family."

I asked, "Can I ask for your permission to take my nieces with me?" He said, "Take them all." But my sister begged me to take only two, and to keep two for her. She said, "They are not going to kill me, just putting me in prison. If you take them all, I will be all alone." She pointed at the girl Sao Sina who was nine years old and the youngest boy, Sao Sitah who was seven years old, and told me to take these two. The two other kids I left there.

Then they took my sister away. That was the last time I ever saw her. And I took the kids to the shed I shared with Pich Dovann's family. Now there were twelve of us, all sleeping on the floor of our one-room shack.

◆○◆

One morning, I was making a delivery on the ox cart with another man named Hon. He and I worked together often making deliveries — he wasn't exactly a Khmer Rouge, but he worked with them and had certain perks, and he was a good guy overall. We came by a rice field, and it looked to be blood red. When we got closer, we saw there were at least a hundred dead bodies spread over this field. We got off the ox cart and walked into the rice patty to check the bodies and see if there was anyone we knew. Fortunately, there wasn't, but there were many bodies of young kids and babies too. There was so much blood everywhere.

We got back on our ox cart and after about half a kilometer we came up to a body in the middle of the road. When we got off to move it out of the way, we found a dead mother with her one-year-old baby next to her, who was still alive, barely. I felt a horrible combination of wanting to cry and at the same time being totally numb, because every day we were surrounded by killing, killing, killing.

When we rolled her over, there fell out of her sarong a small bag of gold and some jewelry. Hon and I split the gold fifty-fifty. Then we discussed what to do about the baby, and finally we decided there was nothing we could do. We just got back on the ox cart and kept going with our delivery, leaving the baby right there in the middle of the road, still breathing. Every Cambodian who made it alive through those years has stories like this to tell.

We had been living in Phnom Arai for over two years, and the Khmer Rouge got to know me. Around the middle of 1977, I was given an opportunity to escape and go hide out in a mountain. I told Pich Dovann not to tell anyone and that I would come back as soon as I could to bring the rest of the family.

Just as Chea Sarak had warned me, the Khmer Rouge was beginning to have its own civil war. The Northwest accused the Northeast of collaborating with the Vietnamese. Our leader of the local Khmer Rouge was named Kuon, and he had heard that the Khmer Rouge was coming from the west to kill him, so he decided to escape. He told a few other Khmer Rouge, including Hon, my partner on the ox cart. Hon knew I was a fighter and that my mind was strong so he convinced them that I should join too. There were eleven of us total, and I was the only one who was not Khmer Rouge.

How long did it take to go up the mountain?

The name of the mountain was Phnom Kravanh, and it took an hour to climb up. There were no towns up there. Just wild animals — I saw some tigers — I got close enough to see their eyes. We saw many elephants, monkeys, and alligators too.

How did you eleven get along?

We got along well because we all escaped together. We came together for one purpose, to avoid getting killed, so we got along.

Were any of the Khmer Rouge you were involved with killing innocent people?

Yes, they were involved in the killing of innocents. But they were also scared. If they didn't follow through with the orders, they too would be killed. So they also were doing what they had to in order to stay alive.

Since Kuon was the leader of the town, he planned his escape ahead and hid guns and food in a warehouse. We began to go down the mountain at night and collect what he hid. This was the first of many trips at night to steal food to survive and run back up the mountain.

Ten days later, all eleven men came down to pick up their families, so very soon there were over a hundred people up in the mountain. I brought Pich Dovann and her entire family, plus my niece and nephew. A month later it grew to thousands of people. Too many to count. And more and more Khmer Rouge soldiers escaped up the mountain, and most had guns with them.

There were probably one hundred armed men up there. So, the Khmer Rouge were too scared to come find us because the terrain was unknown, and we could shoot them from up above.

It was like a small city on top of the mountain. People slept on the ground, or a hammock if they were lucky. We burnt wood for light. We could walk to a stream for drinking and bathing. Everywhere was the bathroom. If people got sick and died, you just left them there — we couldn't even bury people. No ceremony, just leave the body there. We had to keep moving. Our entire life was just running and escaping.

How did people eat up in the mountain?

If you had gold, you could trade for food — half a gram of gold for ten cups of rice. But if you had no gold, you had to steal your own food. We did the night-time raids for food about two or three times per week to steal rice and potatoes from Phnom Arai. We'd sneak into farms and dig up potatoes out of the ground.

This is how it worked — we would go down the mountain before the sun went down and wait at the bottom until dark. Then it was an eight-kilometer walk to Phnom Arai. We would walk there together, but when we got to town, everyone was on their own — just grab what you can and make it back as quickly as possible.

Sometimes two hundred people followed me down — men and women. Other groups of people had gotten stopped at a checkpoint or were all killed by landmines. Most people would say, "Go follow Oum Ry — it's safer." I didn't have any special skills, I just had heart.

I remember one time when I was leading a food raiding mission, we came across a shed that we could see from the outside had many bags of rice inside. I just didn't feel good about it — I think my guardian spirit Ta Kaan was speaking to me, because I just knew something was not right. I yelled at everyone to stand still and not get too close, but some of the people were so eager to grab the rice they ignored me and just ran right into the shed, setting off a trip wire booby trap set by the Khmer Rouge. There was a huge explosion and instantly there were dead people and body parts all over the place. I have no idea how many people were hit, but there were people with missing limbs still alive, screaming and trying to crawl to safety. I couldn't help anybody — all I could do was step over them, grab as much rice as I could and run back up the mountain.

Also, we discovered a community of indigenous mountain

people called the Bunong.[7] They had big earrings and wore small shorts with no shirts, and sometimes we would steal their food at night. Once we killed one of their pigs and chopped it up right there in the field and twenty of us carried pieces of pig back to our camp and fed our families, then sold the rest of the meat to other people up in the mountain.

As the months went on, people began to look up to me as a leader. Thousands of people listened to me. Even Kuon, the leader of Phnom Arai, started to listen to me. The Khmer Rouge people respected me because they were scared of me. Before, I was scared of them, but up on the mountain, they knew everyone would listen to me, so I became the big leader.

How long were people living in the mountain?

We lived up there for eight months. But then someone was able to steal a radio and some batteries from the Khmer Rouge and we began to be able to pick up news at nighttime. We heard news that the Vietnamese army had entered Cambodia and were defeating the Khmer Rouge. But we still stayed up in the mountain because we were scared — we didn't know if there was still Khmer Rouge in power near us, or if the Vietnamese would kill us.

The war was over in January of 1979, but we didn't leave the mountain for three months after that. Finally, the Vietnamese came up the mountain one afternoon, and everyone started running and trying to escape. We thought they were following us to kill us. They yelled, "Don't run, it's okay! We are here to liberate your country!"[8]

The Vietnamese asked who the leader was, and all the people pointed to me. So, they wrote the letter that assigned me as a leader. The next day, thousands of us went down the mountain. It was our first taste of freedom in four years — it was the first time that we were not scared all the time.

We walked for fifteen days, from Phnom Kravanh to Battambang Province. We slept on the side of the road or rested in people's homes. The roads were filled with people, and we began to see the extent of the devastation. There were only a few cars, and all the roads were blocked or disconnected; most of the bridges and train tracks were blown up. And there was no currency, and no government in place.

When we got to Battambang, we all stayed at a coconut plantation. I met so many boxer friends of mine, and we would hug and yell, "We survived!" There was a New Year's celebration, dancing, after a month they organized a traditional Cambodian play called lakhaon. They even were able to import beer from Thailand — it was one of the happiest days of my life — that first sip of cold beer after surviving the Killing Fields, I will never forget how good it tasted.

A few weeks after we arrived in Battambang, by coincidence I met my sister Oum Thouk at a small market. I was ecstatic! At the time I had a lot of gold, mostly from finding it on the dead people I buried and created a hidden pocket in my pants to carry it with me at all times. I gave her three grams to buy a bicycle. My sister and I decided to trade kids. I gave her our sister Oum Sarom's kids and she gave me a different nephew, little Narith, who was the son of my younger brother Rann, who died. When Narith came to live with us, he was probably eleven years old — a good kid, looked like he was from India, very handsome, and quiet.

I was so happy to see my sister, but we didn't talk about our experiences over the last four years. We all survived hell, and we didn't want to talk about it. We just asked who's alive and who died, that's it. If we didn't see someone, we assumed they died. Nobody had time to ask, "Why did this happen?"

This was also the time we first heard the name Pol Pot. We went through four years of Khmer Rouge rule, and we didn't even know the name of the leader. That is how little we understood what was happening to us. And now, no one knew where Pol Pot was. Some said he was deep in the jungle, some said he was in China.

—◆o◆—

When I look back on those years, it is just as confusing now as it was then. Cambodians executed a genocide against their own people. I have never heard of this happening anywhere else in the world, and it breaks my heart every time I think about what happened to our country and our people, and especially the children who were starved and beaten.

For those first couple of months in Battambang, we were able to experience a normal life without constant fear. While drinking beer in Battambang, I met many people. But two would have a big impact on me in the future — a man named Sun would save my life in Siem Reap and another, Prum Deth, would betray me at the 007 Camp.

After living in Battambang for two months, two friends of mine, Troeung Sosay and one of my frequent fighting opponents, Chhit Sarim, told me they are going to be drivers in a convoy of vehicles delivering goods from Thailand to Phnom Penh. I asked if I could come along because I wanted to go try to find my family.

This convoy was huge! There were a hundred cars and trucks, well over a kilometer in length, all packed with food, clothes, everything we couldn't get for four years. The first six trucks in the convoy were just the fuel trucks — because there were no gas stations anymore, you had to always bring your own fuel. People rode on top of the cargo. It took us two full days and two nights to get to the city.

They told me that it would take two days to unload all the cargo and that we would leave back north on the third day. I set out to try to find anyone in my family.

What month did you make it back to Phnom Penh?

I returned to my city in July 1979, but it was nothing like I remembered. The Vietnamese were controlling it, and there were very few Cambodians there at the time. We had no transportation to take us around, so I walked everywhere. There was very little destruction, everything was just boarded up or falling apart from neglect. I wanted to feel happiness for being back, but all I felt was more sadness. It was so quiet and empty, like a ghost town. As I walked to the empty Central Market, the heart of the city where two million people once lived, all of a sudden, I remembered what Yeay Puch told me when I was a child — "There will be an empty city, with empty streets and empty homes." My heart was broken as I walked around the dead city I loved so much.

Everyone knew instinctively that when the war was over, we should go back to where we grew up to find our family. I caught a ride to Kampong Luong, the town we grew up in. I found my brother Oum Sunthon there. He built a little shed and shared as much news as he knew. I asked about our mother and our siblings, but he had no clue. I started crying because I knew I had lost everything — my family, my children, my career, my country. That's why I haven't wanted to go back to Phnom Penh, even until now. It reminds me that I miss my family so much. I don't want to feel that sadness anymore. It was at that moment that I realized that I had to leave Cambodia, and I decided I was going to do everything I could to try to come to America.

6

— Refugee —

How long did you stay with your brother?

I stayed with my brother only three or four hours — I wish I could have stayed longer, but the convoy was headed back up north. I had to make sure to get back on it. I found my friends in car #54 and we headed back to Battambang.

Even though the war was over, things were lawless, and always dangerous. At any point you could run into trouble with the Khmer Rouge, Serey Ka or the Vietnamese army. The three-way war continued, and regular people got stuck in the middle. And there were a lot of revenge killings against the Khmer Rouge soldiers, with knives, axes, anything people could find. Not only were there no laws, there was no currency. The only way you could get food is to trade in gold, and if you had no gold, you had to steal from the people who did.

What was your plan?

I had heard that the U.N. was creating refugee camps on the Cambodian side of the Thai border. I decided that I would go back to Battambang and pick up Pich Dovann and her family and head to the camps to try to emigrate.

But on the convoy ride back, I got very close to being arrested by the Vietnamese. It was another one of those times where I believe my guardian spirit Ta Kaan helped me survive.

The ride was two days, and halfway in the middle we stopped in the town of Siem Reap. The convoy stopped there for people to eat and stretch. I went on a walk and explored a little. When I got back, I heard from people that the Vietnamese army was looking for me, by name, in order to arrest me. I have no idea how they knew I was there, and no idea why they would arrest me. I had just spent most of the last year hiding on top of a mountain. Maybe they thought I was part of Serey Ka? Maybe somebody lied to them about me? Maybe they just wanted to arrest someone famous? I ran out of there as fast as I could and tried to find a safe place to collect my thoughts.

I got a few blocks away from the convoy and was standing on a street corner trying to figure out which direction to go, when all of a sudden, I saw a friend of mine named Sun on a motorbike. He was the boxing fan that I met while drinking beer in Battambang a few months earlier. Back then he told me he lived in Siem Reap and if I was ever in the area to look him up. But somehow, he had found me. He rode up to me and told me to get on the back, that he was working with the Vietnamese and heard that the governor had sent an order to arrest me, so he started riding around town hoping to find me first.

Sun took me to his family's small home behind a Buddhist temple, and they helped me. The first thing they did was cut my hair. My hair was down to the bottom of my back because

I had been living in the mountain for so long. They also gave me a bandanna and a shirt, an old black one, the same as we used to wear under the Khmer Rouge. They were so kind to offer me food too, but I was so nervous, I couldn't eat at all.

I wanted to try to get back on the convoy somehow, but Sun warned me not to go to Battambang — he said that the Vietnamese will call their colleagues there to hunt me down. He told me the town before Battambang was called Svay Sisophon and suggested I go there because it would be close enough to send a message to my family.

I thanked his mother for her generosity and left to go back to the convoy. As I walked out of their home, there was another amazing coincidence — right across the street from the temple was the very beginning of the convoy, the six fuel trucks at the front. It was literally right across the street. My previous car was #54 —half a kilometer away. I went to the first fuel truck to see if I could get a ride on top of it. When I got close, the driver, who I had never seen before, recognized me, even with my short hair, and said, "Oum Ry, climb up for a ride." I climbed up just to find twenty other people catching a ride.

We were set to leave when all of a sudden, the Vietnamese returned, and this time they blocked the road with four of their cars. They pointed their machine guns at the first gasoline truck and yelled, "Where is Oum Ry? We want Oum Ry!" From on top of the truck I quickly yelled back at them, "Oum Ry is in car #54." The soldiers left to go find car #54, but the leader of the squad stayed by the first truck. I had a gold ring, so I gave it to the driver and asked him to bribe the leader of the Vietnamese squad who was blocking our way. The soldier quickly took the ring, and waved the truck through, yelling "Go! Go! Go!" while the rest of the convoy stayed there as they looked for me. We drove for forty-five minutes until we cleared the area and then waited for the rest of the convoy to catch up to us.

I felt so lucky to escape Siem Reap, but I was very scared because I didn't know why they were after me. The fuel truck dropped me off in the outskirts of Svay Sisophon at one a.m., and I snuck into an empty outdoor market area and slept there on a wooden bench.

It was a strange combination to be so desperate and so famous at the same time. Sometimes it worked for me, sometimes against me. But in Svay Sisophon I was really lucky because I was noticed by a boxing fan who helped get me established.

His name was Chea and he noticed me in the market, a few days after I arrived. He invited me to go back to where his family was staying — about two hundred people, a bunch of families who were living together in a sort of compound. It was that night that I first saw Yany. She was so beautiful, I knew I wanted to get to know her. We had just survived four years of war every single day, but when I saw her, it was like she was glowing. She looked like a movie star.

I asked Chea, "Who is that girl standing over there? Is she married or single?" He told me that they killed her husband and her only child starved to death and that she and her girl-friend were trying to make it to the Thai border to emigrate.

How old were you two at the time?

I was thirty-one and she was twenty-six. Everything about her was beautiful — her figure, her face, her hands, every-thing. But she wasn't impressed that I was a famous boxer. She told me she hated boxers. But we got to know each other, and we fell in love very quickly. Our first night together, we stayed up all night talking. It felt so good to be able to connect with someone. After that, I would sing songs to her every night.

A month after we met, I got Yany pregnant. I told her, "If you have a baby with me and become my wife, we will have a future together."

Also, around that time, I met a new friend named Vong and he had a motorbike. I asked him to go to Battambang and find Pich Dovann and my nephew Narith and tell them that I can't come back, but that they should come visit me in Svay Sisophon.

After a month, Pich Dovann and Narith came to visit. Pich Dovann and I had been through so much together, we escaped death so many times, but we arrived at the end of our time together. It is strange to think that when our life was complete hell, she and I loved each other and were a good team. But when the war was over, we quickly drifted apart. She knew that I wanted to go to America, and I knew that she would never leave her mother alone in Cambodia. We had a good conversation — Pich Dovann even met Yany, and Yany gave her a gold necklace as a sign of respect. She left my nephew Narith with me and returned to Battambang that same afternoon. That was the last time I have ever seen Pich Dovann, but I heard she married a minister in the government and wound up having another child and a comfortable life.

This was November 1979. I felt safe in Svay Sisophon, but I kept thinking about how we could get to the border. From the stories I was able to piece together, it seemed like there were seven or eight refugee camps on the Thai border. Some were run by the U.N., and some were run by Serey Ka. The Thai government wanted this large gathering of Cambodians on their border because they thought it would be a buffer if the Vietnamese decided to invade Thailand.

And soon we were in a hurry to leave because a Vietnamese soldier fell in love with Yany. He even said that she reminded him of a famous movie star. I can't blame him because I thought the exact same thing. But if he found out she was pregnant and that we were together, I knew they would arrest and kill me. We quickly set plans to leave the following night at nine p.m. Yany, Narith and I walked for twelve hours until we got to the 007 Camp.

The refugee camp was actually called Nong Samet, but everyone called it 007 because there was so much drama and intrigue there. The camp was run by Serey Ka, "the freedom fighters." But really, they were more like gangsters. In many ways they were similar to the Khmer Rouge, except that they had open markets and used money. If they thought you had a lot of gold on you, they would just kill you and take it.

We arrived at around nine a.m. and looked around for a place to get settled. There were already thousands of people there and no real organization, no place to sign up. For about an hour we walked around to try to figure out what to do when suddenly, I ran into Prum Deth, the boxer I met while drinking beer in Battambang a few months before. He pointed at a building and said to me "I have some beer for you, come with me." But when we got there, all of a sudden, I was surrounded by Serey Ka men with guns pointed at me. I turned to call Prum Deth, but he was gone, totally disappeared. He set me up, and to this day, I don't know why he betrayed me like that.

I was completely surrounded and had nowhere to run. They accused me of being KGB and working with the Vietnamese. I told them that I was just a boxer. "I am Oum Ry," I said. "I came here because I am running away from the Vietnamese."

They didn't care and kept telling me I was KGB.

They took me to a holding cell, which was a barbed wire cage, and handcuffed me to a tree, both hands were behind my back. Soon after that they brought another prisoner, and they handcuffed him to the same tree, my left hand to his right, and his right to my left. He was a gold trader named Kheng — they probably just arrested him to steal his gold.

They left us handcuffed to this tree for three full days. We had no idea how long they were going to hold us for, or if they would kill us at any moment. We would often overhear the Serey Ka soldiers talking about taking us out to kill. On the second night, they came and took Kheng away and left me tied to the tree. I never saw him again.

How did you eat?

The Serey Ka cook worked close by and saw me. She was a trans woman named Bo. She came to me and said, "I know you are Oum Ry," and she brought me food and literally fed me by hand because both my hands were tied behind my back.

If it wasn't for her helping me, I wouldn't have eaten anything because the Serey Ka would never think about that. She even opened my pants and put a plastic bag on me so I could pee.

What were Yany and Narith doing while you were arrested?

Yany helped save me by organizing a protest. Word spread throughout the camp that Oum Ry was there and had been arrested. For three days, people gathered outside the barbed wire cage to come see for themselves. Yany went to find the senior officials of Serey Ka and tell them that I was not KGB. She found the second in command of the whole camp and told him that I was the famous boxer, not working for the Vietnamese.

His name was Chea Chaya and he was a former police officer in Phnom Penh before the war. He came inside the barb wire cage to see for himself. He asked me if I was KGB and I said, "I am only a fighter. I have never met any KGB in my life." Then the next question he asked was if I wanted to join Serey Ka and become his personal bodyguard. I said, "Yes, I am someone you can count on." He ordered me untied and then gave me a gun, and I bowed down to thank him. I went from being a prisoner on the verge of execution to having a powerful position at the top of Serey Ka, literally within a matter of minutes. And it was all because Yany was smart enough and strong enough to save my life.

And soon after that I became head of security for all of Serey Ka. I had thirty or forty people under me that I managed. Our job was just protecting, we were not regular Serey Ka soldiers that would harass and hurt people — our only job was to make sure the leaders were safe. I built a shed behind the house of Chea Chaya and moved my family there, so I was always close by to him. He was a good man, he respected people.

What was life like at the 007 Camp?

It was like a city, there were more than ten thousand people living there. There were restaurants, bars, bands playing, they sold beer — all the things were imported from Thailand.

There was no real organization — you slept wherever you could find a place. If you were by yourself, you would just put up a hammock somewhere. But if you had a family you would have to buy wood to build a shed to sleep in. We built a one room shed and Yany, Narith, and a friend of mine named Sou slept on the floor.

I almost got killed by accident once, and again Yany saved my life. We were at a restaurant in the middle of the camp when a fire fight broke out between Serey Ka and the Khmer Rouge. Yany was seven months pregnant at the time. They were shooting machine guns everywhere and she dove under a table to hide. I was in total shock and just kept standing there, frozen. Then Yany jumped up, grabbed me by the collar and yanked me to the ground. Less than two seconds later a bullet went flying through the exact spot where I was standing — I know this because it hit a water tank that was directly behind me and water started spraying everywhere.

But overall, now that I was working for Serey Ka, I felt much more secure living at the camp, plus I was making a little bit of money. And I had three guns — an AK47, a pistol, and a rocket launcher.

Also, there were a lot of women, and so much fun to have.

And Yany was pregnant at the time?

Yes.

But I thought you said to her that if she had your baby, you two would be together forever?

Yes, I said that. But I never said I wouldn't have other girl-friends. She told me, "I hear stories about you and other women. Don't ever let me see it."

Then one time when she was eight months pregnant, she saw me eating with a sixteen-year-old girl at a noodle shack. I had seen this pretty girl, I don't remember her name anymore, but her father was killed, and she lived with her mother and sister. I wanted to meet her. I offered to help build a shed for her mother. Then I took this girl out to eat, and someone snitched on me and told Yany. While we were eating, I saw her coming straight at us with a big wooden stick in her hands. I told one of my security men to go stop her, turn her around and take her home, so I could continue. Later that afternoon, after the girl and I slept together, I came back to our shed. I knew Yany would be mad, but I didn't realize how mad — she was so furious she tried stabbing me.

A month later, when it came time for Yany to have our baby, I tricked her. I told her that she had to go to another camp called Khao-I-Dang because it was run by the U.N., and they had better doctors. I said, "You must go now while you can get a ride with the U.N. vehicle, and I will come once the baby is born."

Why didn't you want to go with her?

Like I said there were a lot of women there at the time, and I was having too much fun.

But then she tricked me back. Once she was at Khao-I-Dang camp, she sent a messenger to find me and tell me that the baby was born. I packed my things up and went to join her that same night. But when I got there, she was still pregnant. The very next day she gave birth to our first child, a beautiful boy named Narin, which means Black Dragon.

Once our first child was born, I stopped pursuing women. Before Pol Pot, when I was one of the most famous people in Cambodia, all I cared about was fighting and sex. But now, I wanted to be a good father, and to give a good life to my family. I guess you can say that Pol Pot taught me how to be affectionate and how to love people.

We lived at the Khao-I-Dang camp for a full year as we tried to figure out how to get to America. An old friend of mine named Maday Noy heard I was still alive and living at the camp. He came to see me and asked if I could still fight and told me that he could set a paying fight for me. I knew I was going to lose, but I needed the money. I trained a little in front of my shack for a week — I had no bags or sparring partners.

I fought a Thai named Yot Paya in 1980, in Khao-I-Dang camp. This would be my last fight, and in the third round I threw in the towel and said I could no longer continue. I felt that if I kept fighting, I'd have a heart attack. I didn't want a fighting career anymore, I just wanted to take my family to the United States. That's all I thought about.

Around this time, I ran into the brother of Sarith Ban, my

childhood friend from Kampong Luong. He told me that Sarith was still alive and had made it to America already. He told me that Sarith could sponsor me to bring my whole family. He told me in the application that I should write my last name as Ban, so that I could say that I was part of his family. I changed my name from Oum Ry to Oumry Ban.

We filled out the paperwork, and then we had to wait for who knows how long to find out if our paperwork got accepted. They would post the names of people who had gotten selected outside the U.N. office, and every morning, we ran there to see if our names were called. And it's not just America, it was Europe too. One day I saw my name was selected to go to France. Yany said she wanted to go because she had a cousin in Paris, but I said "I don't want to go. If you go, that is fine, but we will separate." Even though I could speak French and didn't know English, I wanted to go to America because when people sent money, the U.S. dollar is what everyone wanted.

A few months later, two important things happened — Yany got pregnant for a second time, and we were told that we were selected to come to the United States. But first we would go to the Philippines to live in another camp, while our paperwork was being processed. We wound up living in the Philippines for about eight months and that is where our daughter was born, so we named her Manila, after the capital city.

How did it feel leaving Cambodia, knowing you may never come back?

It's very clear that I am one of the lucky ones. I was picked by a guardian angel to stay alive — I really think Ta Kaan was there for me when I needed him most. So many people I have known have died. So many times, I almost died. As the plane took off, I looked out the window and I remember feeling, "Maybe it's been chosen that I should be alive?"

7

—◆— America —◆—

When did you arrive in the United States?

December 1980. We flew from the camp in the Philippines
straight to Chicago — Yany, my nephew Narith, and our two
kids, Narin and Manila. We were sponsored by a man named
Michael Stanke.

*I thought you were getting sponsorship from your child-
hood friend Sarith Ban?*

I thought so too, and I even changed my legal name on the
immigration papers to "Oumry Ban," but then they told us
that someone else sponsored our arrival. Mr. Stanke was
an unmarried man, a pastor, around fifty years old, and he
sponsored twenty families to come to the Chicago area. They
didn't give us any choice, but we were happy to go anywhere

because our goal was to come to the United States, it didn't matter where we ended up.

Mr. Stanke helped rent homes for all the families he sponsored but for some reason, he decided my family would live with him in his home on the Southside of Chicago. When we landed at the airport, he had a sign with my name on it and I bowed down to him. At the time, Yany and I knew little to no English, but fortunately he spoke some French, so we were able to talk a little.

The very first day when we landed, the snow was up to my knees. I had never seen snow before, and it was a type of cold I never imagined. But no matter how cold it got, I always thought, "Anywhere is better than Pol Pot."

After we had been there for two weeks, a Cambodian friend who lived close by came to visit, and we decided to walk to the store to buy some beer. It was about a kilometer away, but it was December in Chicago, and it was minus ten degrees outside. There were warnings for people not to go out, but for some reason we thought it was a good idea to walk, or at least we didn't think it was a bad idea. But by the time we got there, both of our feet had become numb from the cold. The liquor store owner asked us why we were walking, but our English wasn't good enough to answer. We bought a six pack of cold beer and he called the police, who picked us up to take us home. I was used to the authorities during the Khmer Rouge who could kill you at any moment — it was a new experience to see police who actually helped people.

How long did you stay with Mr. Stanke?

We lived with him for two years. He was a very kind man and did so much to help us.

Tell me about Sarith, what happened to him?

When we were young, Sarith trained with me for a while, but he quit because he said he "didn't enjoy the pain." I wanted us to train together. In 1970, Sarith joined the army to defend Cambodia and push the Vietcong out. He was on the front line. When he was training in Kampong Speu (about one hundred miles away from Phnom Penh), the Khmer Rouge entered the city. He managed to flee to Thailand in 1978, and was held as a prisoner for a bit because they accused him of being a part of the Khmer Rouge. He was one of the first wave of Cambodians who got into the Thai refugee camps.

Sarith was sponsored by a family in San Francisco and arrived in October 1978. But the family who sponsored him never showed up. He was then sponsored by another family in Twin Peaks. He stayed with them for about a year before moving to Southern California in 1980, where he met his wife, Chhom Sao, and took ESL classes. They have two sons and a daughter. He's mostly retired now, but he worked various jobs such as construction work and making donuts. His favorite song to play during work hours was "Stayin' Alive" by the Bee Gees.

How did you go about learning English?

I told the pastor I wanted to go to school, but he told me if I wanted to learn English, the best thing would be to get a job and learn while working and earning money at the same time.

He brought me to work at a restaurant nearby as a dishwasher. They paid me three dollars and seventy-five cents an hour and I worked forty hours a week. At that time, Yany wasn't working because she had to take care of the babies. And soon she was pregnant again with our third child, who we named Unite.

When we saved enough money, we got our own apartment uptown, in a Cambodian neighborhood that had Khmer markets and restaurants. And I was able to get a job cleaning rooms in a big hotel in the middle of Chicago called The Palmer House. I took the train and a bus there every day. It was twenty-five floors and there were over three hundred people working there to keep the hotel in good shape. They paid me five dollars an hour. When I first started, I couldn't finish the eighteen rooms I was assigned. I almost cried and thought, "There is no way I can do this," but the supervisor told me to not worry. A month later, I became so much faster. I grew to love that job. Cleaning is like my therapy, it relieves stress for me. I worked from eight to five, five days a week. And Mr. Stanke was right, I started learning English through "on-the-job-training."

Was it hard to learn?

It wasn't too hard because I studied the basic alphabet and grammar. The pronunciation was different and sometimes difficult, but I could read English very well. I can only hear from one ear which sometimes made it more complicated. But for some reason, if women talk to me, I can hear fine.

And after the shift at the hotel, I had a second job as a security guard for a Cambodian gambling house. These games were not legal, so the owners couldn't call the cops if there was a problem, and since I was a famous fighter, they gave me fifty dollars a day to watch over the games.

I would stay there until whenever they finished gambling, oftentimes they'd play until the next morning. I would go from the hotel to the casino back to the hotel in the morning, and there were many times I barely slept, but I was happy because I was in America with my family, and making money, which was my dream.

Eventually, I hired an old Cambodian woman to look after the kids. Yany also got a job at a diner. We were able to save and buy our first car — a used 1980 Buick Skylark. Once we had the car, we began exploring the Great Lakes and the surrounding states, visiting friends in Michigan and Indiana.

How were you and Yany getting along?

We were good, we never fought. I stopped being a playboy. I saw that my wife was beautiful and we were raising our children together. We were putting our new life in America together, but we were both still haunted by what we lived through during the Pol Pot years. I had nightmares most nights, rarely did I have good dreams. Often, I dreamt I was still living on the mountain. Some nights, I dreamt the Khmer Rouge were trying to kill me. Yany had nightmares too, but we didn't talk about them. I told her we should stop thinking about Cambodia.

But then Yany heard rumors that I was having an affair with the young daughter of my boss at the casino. I wasn't, but she didn't believe me. And within two weeks, she decided that she wanted the family to move to California. I was against this idea because I loved my jobs in Chicago and I was saving money to buy a house. Also, my friends at the casino warned me not to move because we'd probably break up. They told me when their friends moved, their marriages fell apart because there were too many Cambodian women in California. I was afraid I might go back to my womanizing ways. Chicago is not a place for fun — just work, make money and stay home. I told her not to move there, but she replied, "I am going to California and taking the kids with me. You can stay here alone in Chicago if you want."

I didn't think she was serious until one morning I came home at eight a.m. after being at the casino all night, and I saw our car was packed with almost everything we owned. Clothes, pots and pans, even our color TV. She said, "I'm serious. We are moving to California. Are you coming or not?"

I ran upstairs and packed the few things I owned in ten minutes and came back down. The rest of our stuff we gave to our neighbors. I told Yany, "If you are moving, I am moving too." In case I wouldn't go, Yany recruited our friend Sam to make the trip with her. The seven of us, with everything we owned, packed into the Buick and started driving — Sam and I in the front, Yany, with the new baby on her lap, our two other kids and my nephew all fit in the back.

We asked people how to get to California and they said, "Just go on Highway 80."

Did you have a map?

No map. And even if we had one, we wouldn't be able to read it. We just got in the car and started driving west. If we couldn't read the signs, we pulled over to ask for directions.

The drive was three days and three nights. The first night we slept in Des Moines, Iowa. Then the next night was Rock Springs, Wyoming. Then Reno, Nevada. We even put country music on the radio as we drove through. It was beautiful seeing the Western States. It was just like the Clint Eastwood movies I used to watch in Phnom Penh. The colors and the vastness of the landscape filled me with wonder and awe, and I began to get excited for our new beginning.

Did you have any car problems?

No troubles at all. From Wyoming to Utah there was a huge storm, and it wouldn't stop raining. All the other cars raced past us, but we moved like a turtle, slow and steady.

But we almost had a horrible accident. One rainy night when Sam was driving in Wyoming, he almost drove the car over a cliff. We had pulled over to pee, and we were in the middle of nowhere. It was pitch black outside. When he tried to get back on the freeway, Sam made a wrong turn and got us lost. I kept telling him to turn around, but he was so confident that he knew what he was doing, even though in the rain we could barely see ten feet in front of us. All of a sudden, I had a bad feeling, and I yelled at him to slam on the brakes. Fortunately, he did, and I jumped out of the car to get a better view. That's when I noticed we were five feet away from a cliff that was at least a two-hundred-foot drop. I cussed out Sam, "You idiot! I told you to turn the other away! You could've killed us!"

How did you know to yell stop?

I don't know. I just felt it. It was another one of those moments that I felt my guardian spirit Ta Kaan was there to help me. We were just seconds away from all dying and maybe nobody would ever find us.

What happened when you finally got to California?

I had a friend in San Jose, but we didn't know where San Jose was or how to get there. When we finally arrived in Sacramento, I called him from a pay phone, and he gave me the directions to get to his house.

Once we were there, they helped us find a place to rent close to them in San Jose. We rented a one-bedroom apartment for seven hundred dollars for seven people. Yany was very happy, but I wasn't. My heart was still in Chicago, and I told her I wanted to go back because I wanted to work. But soon I was able to find more work doing security for a Cambodian gambling house, making fifty dollars per day, and they also fed me and gave me a place to sleep.

If you were sleeping at work, how often did you manage to see your kids?

Almost every night. I asked my boss for permission to check on my wife and children. And soon Yany was pregnant with our fourth child, a girl we named Calina, for California. She was born in August of 1987.

Were you two planning for another baby?

All our kids were all accidents. We never talked about it ahead of time.

I grew to enjoy life in San Jose. Some days, I made as much as two hundred dollars at the casino and I saved almost five thousand dollars. Yany had a part time job, and I loved being with my kids. In many ways, I was very happy. But at the same time, I still had nightmares from the war. I dreamt about how they tied me, handcuffed me, how they treated me. Sometimes the memories would just flood me, even if I was driving. I often went to Santa Cruz, alone, to the beach, and would cry thinking about Cambodia and my mother and my children, wondering who was still alive? I kept thinking, "Why am I still alive?"

After we had settled in San Jose for a year or so, I called my childhood best friend Sarith Ban. He was living with his family in Long Beach, which was about four hundred miles south.

In February 1987, Yany and I drove down to visit. When we pulled up, Sarith was waiting for me outside on the sidewalk. The last time we saw each other was when we both joined the army in 1970, seventeen years before. His wife cooked dinner for us, and we drank beer and talked all night. We were talking about the early sixties, when we had so much fun when we would sell bread in the summer; we talked about our old friends, who was still alive, who died, and how he escaped. It was so emotional; we cried and laughed many times that night.

The next day, Sarith drove me around Long Beach and showed me the city. He took me to meet his friend named Paline, who was a big boxing fan and had seen me fight many times in Cambodia. He also had a lot of money because he was good with business. I didn't realize this at the time, but this was all part of Sarith's plan — for me to meet Paline, and for Paline to help me start a gym to teach Cambodian Pradal Serey to a new generation.

8

—◆— Long Beach —◆—

Did you ever dream you would have your own gym?

No, never.

How did this all come to be?

I visited Long Beach for the first time in November 1986. I drove back down a few months later to visit Sarith a second time. He suggested we meet Paline again at the Cambodian restaurant called Pagoda. And it was at that second meeting with Paline that he brought up the idea. We talked about all the times he saw me fight in Phnom Penh and that everyone loved me because my style was so unique. We talked about how so many of our famous fighters were killed by the Khmer Rouge, and how important it is to teach the art to a new generation. And finally, he said, "I want to give you the money to start a gym to teach Pradal Serey."

Paline was a translator and owned a business doing voice-overs for Cambodian movies. He was very successful and wanted to do something to help the Khmer people in Long Beach.

I told him I'd be so happy if he opened a gym for me, and I promised him I'll make the gym something the Cambodian people would be proud of. He said he could invest twenty thousand dollars at the beginning and told me to do whatever I thought was best.

After that second meeting with Paline, I went back to San Jose. He called me a few days later saying they found a building. I drove back down a few weeks later and checked it out. It was an old laundry mat, totally gutted, with big holes in the walls and the floors where all the water pipes used to be.

It was owned by a church, and they ran a shelter in the building behind us, so the area had a lot of homeless people. But it was fifteen-hundred square feet and only seven hundred dollars a month. That's how it happened, all in six months. I stayed there and told Yany I was moving to Long Beach to open a gym.

What did Yany say about it?

She was generally supportive, but the kids were in school, and she didn't want to move them down yet. I would drive up every two weeks and spend two or three days with the family.

And when I was in Long Beach, I just slept at the gym. When I needed to shower, I would go to Sarith Ban's house.

Help me understand what was going on in your head when setting up the gym.

At the start, I just copied the gym I trained at when I was young, The Royal Club. We needed carpet and mirrors and some lockers. The hardest part was making the giant metal beams that hold the kicking bags — Paline had to hire a welder to come make it right here.

There were four or five of us working on it, building everything by hand. I was so happy for this opportunity and have my friends who helped me. I'm very grateful.

For the first two years we didn't have a boxing ring, we just fought on the carpet. But then my friend Tippana went to a traditional boxing gym and asked to look at their ring, and under it too, and took all the measurements of every part of it. We copied it and built it inside our gym with just six hundred dollars' worth of materials. This ring has been used almost every day for the last thirty-five years, and it is still in great shape.

What was it like for you to become a teacher? How did you develop your teaching philosophy?

My instructors never taught me how to teach. I invented my own style. I taught everything from the traditional Cambodian style — how to kick, how to block, etc. But I also combined it with things I learned and invented over the years. Like when I was in the army, I went to study close combat — I learned how to stab, how to grab someone's gun, and other techniques. I invented some ways to protect yourself when you get hit. That is separate from boxing in the ring, but I combined it. Someday, I'll write a whole book about it!

If you are going to run a boxing gym, you need to be able to teach thirty beginners at the same time, and also have the skills to coach your competition fighters, one-on-one, in advanced techniques and strategy. If you want to make a name for yourself and your gym, you must produce champions. I can tell when someone has the potential for being a great fighter. You can tell when the fighting comes from their heart. You can be as strong and quick as you can be, but if you have no heart, you have nothing.

What are the mental skills that a person needs to be a good fighter?

I would say the two most important things are desire and focus. A fighter really needs to want to train hard, to take it seriously and to desire being a champion. Everyone knows what focus is, but few people can actually do it. The fighter must not be easily distracted by the crowd, the sounds, the girls, nothing. Some people are just born with the ability, but it is also something that can be practiced through meditation.

Also, a smart practice routine and a good diet are very necessary. And you must manage your personal life to make sure you stay in balance. For instance, a fighter should not have sex for at least a week, maybe two, before a fight, because it makes you lose too much energy. It is important to have the right balance in life — too much sex makes you weak, but not enough sex makes your mind and body feel crazy. A balanced life is really important in order to be the best fighter. If you lose your balance, you will lose your focus and you will lose in the ring.

Who were your first students?

For the first year, it was only Cambodians. At the time, there was a big problem of Mexican gangs picking on Cambodian kids, and beating them up really bad, and then yelling, "Go back to China!" A lot of Cambodian moms brought their children to the gym for them to learn how to fight back.

At the beginning, we had about twenty students and there were only a few that I knew would become good fighters.

And I was also disappointed because I wanted students who were not just Cambodians. Back in 1987, Americans only knew Karate and Tae Kwon Do. There were no Muay Thai or Pradal Serey gyms. Nobody had heard of it. And unfortunately, we didn't have the money to advertise or promote the gym because we were very poor.

But building the ring wound up being very good for business because it made the gym look and feel bigger, and more real. When non-Cambodians saw it, they had much more interest in joining.

Who was the first champion you produced?

That would be Moun Samath. He came in 1987, when he was eighteen years old. In 1990, he became a champion in the International Kickboxing Association. His legs were very fast and sharp. He was a great kicker. All the Thai fighters were scared of him. When he fought at the Hollywood Park casino, he kicked his opponent so much he couldn't walk. He became famous in Long Beach because he won three championships — the American championship, the IKBA, and California state competition.

What made him really a champion wasn't just his natural talent but also his work ethic. Nobody trained harder than Moun Samath. Other fighters train and want a crowd of people around to cheer them on. But Moun Samath kept quiet and focused, and practiced three hours a day minimum. Often he practiced from morning to night. And I opened the gym for him to come train whenever he wanted — the champions didn't pay for classes, but they did help train others for free.

I want to mention Ron Smith, who joined the gym in 1991. He had more experience with traditional American boxing than Pradal Serey, but he studied and learned quickly and soon became my right-hand man running the gym. Many days he is here twice a day, running the morning and afternoon classes, which really helps me a lot. Over the years, Ron has become a real brother to me.

When a student came in wanting to learn Muay Thai, what would you tell them?

Pradal Serey is the name for Cambodian kickboxing, but nobody knew what it was. Not a lot of people came in. More people were familiar with the name Muay Thai, so I changed the gym name to Long Beach Muay Thai. When students registered, I would tell them "I am not Thai, I am Cambodian, but it is the same fighting." But a couple years went by, and I decided that I wanted to emphasize this as a Cambodian art, so I changed the sign back to Pradal Serey.

And let me tell you something else — because we are right next door to a shelter, our block is full of homeless people. For the last thirty years, I've let homeless people sleep at the gym almost every night — but rarely more than two at a time. They sleep in the office or under the ring. Sometimes I have to clean vomit in the morning, sometimes they fight. One time a guy broke the window in the middle of the night and set the gym on fire! The fire department came but not before the walls, floor and weight lifting equipment were damaged — thankfully they got there in time before the ring was ruined. I know it's not good for business and some people may choose to train at a different gym, but helping people keeps me calm. And I have suffered so much in the past that I want to help people if I can.

When did Yany and the kids finally join you in Long Beach?

It was two years later, 1988. Yany got more interested in moving when she found out that there were many job opportunities in Long Beach. Narin was eight years old, Manila was seven, Unite was four and Calina was one. Narith, my nephew, didn't move to Long Beach because when he was eighteen, he met a girl and they moved to Minnesota where he became a pastor, and they have two kids.

When the family finally moved, we found a two-bedroom apartment on 69th St in North Long Beach. I was happy to see my kids and be with my wife again. I bought a van for Yany, and she found a job driving patients to a medical clinic.

How did you and Yany handle it when you both were working and had small children?

We depended on the neighbors to watch out for them. Whatever problems happened, they would call us.

How did it feel having your family back and having a new family at the gym?

I was happy. Narin was a quiet but kind kid, definitely a mama's boy. Manila was a very smart kid, a very serious student, and humble. Unite was talented at drawing from a very young age and would eventually grow up to be a successful businessman. And Calina was so easy to get along with, she was naturally funny and outgoing.

But the business wasn't doing well. That created a lot of stress between me and Yany.

After three years, Paline sat me down one day and told me his business was way down and he had no more money. He told me he will leave the gym to me, but he can no longer support me. I felt sad and scared, and I thanked him for supporting me. He put in fifty thousand dollars over three years to make this happen. I needed to get a job to pay for the gym. I worked as a supervisor for the Yellow Pages phone book, managing three drivers and distribution for the city of Long Beach. I made one hundred dollars a day. It was good money, but then after a few months, my car broke down because I drove so much.

Once Paline could no longer help, the next two or three years were very hard. That's when my wife had to carry the financial weight — 1990, '91, '92, we had no money. There was only enough to pay the rent and utilities.

And to be honest with you, I don't know what ten thousand dollars looks like. I never had ten thousand dollars my whole life. I only had a few thousand. But my wife knew how to make money. She's smart — she just knows how. Yany wasn't happy because the gym hadn't picked up yet and she would say, "If you have a business and it's not making any money, it isn't a business." But I told myself I must continue. Whatever problems I had with the family, my gym was the priority. I promised Paline I would take care of this gym until I die. People spent money on me, and I can't let them down. It breaks my heart just thinking of that.

But business started picking in the middle of 1992 because of three things — the LA Riots*, the popularity of Mixed Martial Arts, and we got discovered by the Hispanic community in this neighborhood. After the riots, people wanted to learn to fight and defend themselves. We got a lot of new students. At the same time, in the early '90s, Gracie Jiu Jitsu became popular. And the MMA tournaments started. And to win at that, you needed to be able to do stand-up work like Pradal Serey but you also needed a ground game that Brazilian Jiu Jitsu is perfect for. Knowing the two is a very powerful combination and that brought a lot of publicity and people wanting to try it. And then Mexicans in Long Beach discovered kickboxing. When I started in 1987, it was all Cambodians, but by 1992, the biggest group of students were Mexican.

A lot of them were gang members. I noticed some of them had the tattoos and they'd throw their gang signs. But they

* Civil disturbances after the acquittal by a mostly white jury of four white police officers who brutally beat Rodney King, an unarmed African American motorist.

respected me. They respect me more than Cambodian kids. Sometimes the Cambodian kids would come in and not even acknowledge me or talk to me. Very soon I would produce three Mexican champs at the gym — Carlos Garcia in 1995, Jose Fernandez in 1996, and Victor Aguilera in 1998. They have better hands, but Cambodians are better with their legs and knees. Mexican fighters didn't use their legs as much as the Cambodian students.

It's amazing that at the beginning Cambodian moms brought their sons to the gym to protect themselves from the Mexican gangs, and later the Mexican students were more respectful than the Cambodians.

Yes, that's exactly what happened.

With business picking up, was Yany feeling better?

Yany and I had our problems, it was complicated. I was jealous of Yany. A couple years after moving to Long Beach she opened a clinic with a doctor and was making very good money. When she started making more money, I felt like she stopped caring about me like before. Then I had an affair — with your mother, Mony — that's when things really began to unravel.

How did the affair happen?

One day, I went to a restaurant called the Chinese King BBQ and she was a waitress there at the time. This was the summer of 1997. Some mutual friends introduced us, and they said I was the famous boxer. She put her fists up in the air, and the first thing she said to me was that she wanted to fight. I should have seen that as a sign of what was to come...

Mony was beautiful and tall and had long hair. But she was tough. Once when she worked at a restaurant and some guy slapped her ass, she back-kicked him to the wall. She still likes to tell people that if she was a man, she'd be the godfather of all the gangs.

Then about a month later, I went to the Siem Reap restaurant with Sarith Ban, and she was now working there. Sarith reminded her that we had once met, and he lied to her and said I had a lot of money. Also, at the time Yany had given me a seven-thousand-dollar diamond ring as a gift. And when I wore that ring, women noticed it. This was in 1997. I was in my fifties and she was in her late twenties.

We got to know each other better after that. She asked me if I had a wife and I told her I did, but we were in the middle of breaking up. She was straight up with me and told me she had a husband in Cambodia, but they were also breaking up, which is why she came to the United States alone. She was just a child during the war years in Cambodia, and she suffered a lot — she still has a huge scar that runs down her entire back from when the Khmer Rouge beat her.

When did it officially end between you and Yany?

Around that time, 1997. Yany hired a private investigator to follow me around for a year. She paid him to spy on me and report back to her if I was fooling around. Which I was, so she had a lot of photos of me. She once told me, "You cannot hide from me, I can find you anywhere." I was renting another apartment, and Yany found out where it was and came over. She was so angry I was having an affair, she picked up my big color TV all by herself and threw it out the second story window.

And around that time, Mony got pregnant.

She didn't want to have a baby and decided to take care of it herself. One time I saw her get on top of a ladder and jump down to the ground, over and over, hoping that would work. I didn't know she was pregnant at the time. I watched her but had no idea why she was doing that. Another time she came to the gym to spar and got in the ring and purposely allowed herself to get kicked in the stomach, twice.

One day her sister and brother-in-law came to the gym and asked me to convince her to keep the baby. Her answer was, "I hate you," but she reluctantly agreed.*

I thought our baby would be born blind or with no legs or some deformity, but nothing was wrong with you. When you were born in September of 2000, you were so beautiful. 2000 is a special year to me because it is the year of the dragon and I consider that to be lucky. We named you Sochada, because in Khmer "Socha" means honesty, and "Da" is a good deed.

And you were so smart. You started training in Pradal Serey when you were five years old. You really grew up in the gym. And I never really trained you, you observed everyone and absorbed knowledge. You are like me when I was younger! Your legs are very fast, and you are an excellent kicker. But I didn't want to teach you too much. I don't want you to become a professional fighter, because it really can mess up your face. I'm definitely proof of that.

What were the early years like?

At the beginning, we lived together to raise you, but she left — she only wanted to go gambling and talk with her

---

* My mother's version of the story is similar. She adds, "I had only been in the United States for two and a half months. I didn't speak any English. I didn't want to have a kid with Oum Ry because he was too old and had another family. I didn't want to interfere. He had serious anger issues, and we were so poor. But he is a very good person. He has a good heart. You were an accident, kuon. I'm very happy I have you though. I cried so much when you were born because I was overwhelmed with emotions. I was so relieved that I gave birth to a girl because I did not want to have a boy. Your dad too. You are so beautiful and look just like me. {laughs} I'm glad you have my height and shape. The only thing I would change about you are your chicken eyebrows, your dad has them too."

friends and family on the phone in Cambodia — one time our phone bill was almost two thousand dollars.* I ended up doing most of the work. I got you breakfast and took you to school, then would go open the gym for the morning training. Then I would pick you up from school, and you trained at the gym with all the men. At the end of the day, I would take you home and order some take out because I am a bad cook. I have many kids, but you are the only one I actually raised every day.

I was very happy — maybe the most happy I had ever been. I loved living in Long Beach, I loved training people at the gym, and I loved taking care of my daughter. I have eight kids, but unfortunately, it took me a long time to figure out how to be a good father. I feel bad about it, but I was too busy training, or working, or having fun. I definitely have regrets. But now I work hard every day, trying to do the right thing for the people in my life.

Another amazing thing that happened around that time was that I found out my son Oum Pee, who was born to Khou Kimny in 1970, survived the war and was still alive in Cambodia, with seven children of his own. My brother randomly met him, and they realized he was my son. Both my wives and my two other children all disappeared, and almost certainly were killed during the war. I was so happy to find out he was still alive! We talk on the phone, and I send him a couple hundred dollars a month. I have resisted going back to Cambodia ever since I left, there are too many painful and heartbreaking memories. But I haven't seen Oum Pee since the Khmer Rouge took over in 1975, and it is a dream of mine to see him with my own eyes and to tell him I love him.

---

* My mother now laughs about this. They had a big fight, which turned physical and then she threw a knife at him. But luckily, as my father puts it, "she has terrible aim." She says she had no idea what those calls cost until after a whole month of being so happy not to be isolated and feeling connected to all the people she missed back home.

9

◆ Attack ◆

Let's talk about the time you were attacked in Long Beach by the Cambodian gang.

It was November of 2006. But I had been living with gangs since I first arrived in 1986. Because I have this gym, I have a unique perspective of gang culture — I have many students who are gang members, and many others who are police. On any given day, they were here together, training at the same time. Both the cops and the gang members trusted me, and I heard many stories.

Back in the early nineties, one of my police students told me that there were seventy different gangs in Long Beach and over eleven thousand members — in a city of four hundred thousand people. One year there were over a hundred gang killings — that's two a week. Long Beach was like a war zone those days.

When the Cambodian population started settling in Long Beach after the war, in the late seventies, the Mexican gangs got territorial and didn't like the new people coming in, and like I mentioned earlier, they would ambush and beat down Cambodian kids, sometimes five versus one, and yell at them to "Go back to China!"

In the early eighties, Cambodian kids started their own gangs. They copied the model of the Mexican gangs that were tormenting them. They did this to protect themselves, but also the gang offered structure and support that a lot of our young people needed, since so many families were damaged in the war.

There were two main Cambodian gangs — Tiny Rascal Gang and Azian Boys, and they fought each other. They also terrorized their own Cambodian community. My friend Tippana had a Khmer restaurant and a Cambodian gang told him he needed to pay five hundred dollars a month for protection, or "something bad might happen." He refused, and two days later they shot out his windows. When he got the windows replaced, two days later they were shot out again. This happened to all our small Cambodian businesses in Long Beach.

The main rival of the Cambodian gangs was the Mexican gang called East Side Longos. And in 1990, the Mexican Mafia ordered West Side Longos to put aside its rivalry with the East Side and support each other, so all the Hispanic gangs were united in their war against the Cambodians.[9] That's when the violence really spiked. The Cambodians in Long Beach were being hit from all directions. Every night you would hear gunfire, sirens, and helicopters. Cambodian kids knew not to go out alone after dark. One family I know, the gang was chasing their son, and he was able to run back home, but the gang broke into their apartment and shot the boy right in front of his parents.

We had escaped one war zone and landed in a different one. There is no way out. When a Mexican kid shoots a Cambodian kid, they can escape to Tijuana. Cambodian people had nowhere else to go. We restarted our lives here — we raised our children here. Where do we go from here? We can't put our backpack on again.

How much direct experience did you have with any of these gangs?

In 1999, the head probation officer for the city of Long Beach approached me about teaching kickboxing to gang members on parole. From all kinds of gangs — Black, Cambodian, Mexican, Japanese, everything. They thought it could teach them discipline and give them a healthy sense of community. They paid ten thousand dollars a year, for forty kids per year, ages between fourteen and eighteen, three times a week.

How was it teaching the gang members?

At first when they walked into the gym, they acted all macho and hard, like they were in jail. But I taught them how to be respectful and show respect. Because when they saw that I respected them, they felt good about respecting me.

They all got along while they were in the gym. Also, they knew if they caused any problems, I'd just tell the prohibition officer and they'd go back to jail.

Since I arrived in 1986, I've lived with gangs all around me. And I never had any problems. Except for the one time I was attacked and almost killed by my own people.

Can you tell me how that night started?

Yes, it was a Saturday night. I went out to dinner with two friends, Nan and Klot, to a Cambodian karaoke restaurant called Bamboo. I remember not feeling good about going there, and I told my friends that we should go somewhere else, but they convinced me to go to Bamboo anyway.

When we walked in there, it was just the owner and a waitress, one couple sitting alone in the corner, and at a big round table there were eight gang members eating together, six men and two women, all in their thirties and forties.

As soon as I walked in, one of them called me "Bou," which means uncle in Khmer, and asked for me to sit with them. But I told him I was meeting friends and went to sit at a table that was just about six feet from theirs. They all knew me, but I only knew a few of them. One of the men, his brother used to train at my gym. And one of the women I knew because her mother had a thing for me.

We sat down and ordered the food and beer. They ate next to us, and everything was perfectly normal. But they were getting louder, and they'd often step outside to smoke, what I am not sure.

Around nine-thirty p.m., I got up and walked over to the owner to pay for our food. The head gang member tried to kick me, but I was able to move out of the way and he completely missed. I was startled and asked, "Why are you starting problems with me?" He began yelling about my former girlfriend — that she went to the police and reported that the gang robbed her apartment. I told him, "Your problem is with her. Go talk to her." Before things could escalate between us, the owner of the restaurant came in between us and said, "No fighting in the restaurant. If you want to fight, take it outside."

I began to walk back to my table when the woman at their table grabbed a stereo speaker and tried throwing it at my head, but it landed right in my chest. I was in shock, it happened so fast. That's when all hell broke loose — the head of the gang began to chase Nan, who ran to the bathroom and locked the door. Klot ran to the other side of the restaurant and hid under a table, while another gang member joined the girl and tried to fight me.

Where was the owner during all this?

He was standing there watching everything unravel. Then, out of nowhere, another one of the gang members yelled that police were on their way. They quickly ran out of the restaurant. I thought it was all over. We stayed at our table for a while, trying to stay calm, and waited for them to leave. Even to this day, I think what my grandmother Yeay Puch told me — "Be calm, be kind, be brave." Once we paid our bill, I looked out the window and it looked like they had all driven off. I told my friends we could go home now, and we began walking out of the restaurant, with me going out first.

Two steps after going outside, all of a sudden, I got hit in the back of the head with a crowbar. They had been hiding and waiting for me to come outside. I fell face first and got knocked unconscious. Then my friends said three of the gang members started kicking me in the head and all over my body — like a soccer ball. It was the gang leader, the other aggressive one, and the woman who threw the radio at my chest. She was particularly angry and was stomping on my face with her high heels.

I was unconscious on the ground. I don't remember anything. I was told all this because Klot and Nan watched from inside the restaurant. They didn't dare come outside because they were afraid. And the owner refused to call the police.

Why?

The owners and my friends were afraid of revenge from the gangs. Fortunately, the couple that was sitting alone in the back weren't scared because they were from San Jose and they finally called the police.

But before the cops came, they continued to beat me in the parking lot right in front of the restaurant for almost ten minutes. Toward the end, the woman took a rope and tied it around my neck. They began to attach it to the back of their truck so they could drive off. Feeling the rope around my neck somehow woke me up, and I tried to open my eyes, but they were too swollen and covered in blood.

Right when I needed them the most, the police arrived. As soon as the sirens were heard, the gang got in their cars and escaped. If the police were a minute later, I am sure I would have been dead.

I really believe it was my guardian spirit Ta Kaan that helped me again that night. There were so many times I got close to being killed — when the Vietnamese tried to arrest me, when Serey Ka accused me of being KGB, when the boobytrap blew up all the people when we were stealing rice, when my friend Sam almost drove my entire family off a cliff in Wyoming... and now this. Every time, I believe Ta Kaan was there to help me.

Klot and Nan came out to the parking lot and carried me inside. They propped me up on a chair. I was having trouble breathing. I touched my face and there was so much blood, pouring out of my eyes and nose and mouth. I remember waking up briefly and passing out again. The next time I woke up, I was in the hospital.

What time did you get to the hospital?

I got to the emergency room at eleven p.m., and all night long people were coming to visit me. They were all crying, and it was the first time I felt important to people. I thought, "Wow, people really do love and care about me. I've never felt this before." Some friends joked with me and said, "Oh my God! We thought you were dead already." I laughed and said, "It takes a lot more work to kill me."

There must have been a hundred people who came to visit me in the middle of the night. The hospital asked "Who are you? Why are so many people visiting you?" By six a.m., they had discharged me. I had a friend who was working as security at the hospital who later told me that they discharged me so early because they were overwhelmed by the number of people trying to visit me.

When did you first realize what they did to your face?

When they discharged me and I went to Yany's house in North Long Beach, I touched my face, and it was so swollen. My face was fractured in three places — my cheekbones, the right side of my jaw, and my forehead. I could not open my mouth. The swelling went down after a week, but I still had scars and bruises. The doctor told me, "You might have problems with your sight because you were bleeding so much from your eyes." He told me I didn't need surgery for anything, to just let it naturally heal, maybe six to eight months.

It took about a year for my body to feel back to normal. I don't have trouble chewing anymore, but my eyesight still has some damage to this day.

When I was at Yany's house, everyone gave me money. I counted it up, and I almost had eight thousand dollars. I wrote a thank you card to everyone. A Cambodian newspaper published my story, as well as the *Long Beach Press-Telegram*.

Three nights after the attack, my friend Tippana organized a community meeting to discuss what was happening with the gangs within the Cambodian community in Long Beach. He made flyers and phone calls, and there were eighty people who came to the meeting at the Mark Twain Library. I didn't go because I didn't feel well yet. The Long Beach detectives came and listened to everyone.

There were students of mine — both police and gang members — who were there that night, and they told the detectives, "You better find these people quickly, before we find them." The next morning, the three detectives came to Yany's house with photos of gang members for me to identify.

The police decided to put a detail on me to make sure the gang wouldn't come back. The police worked hard, and found the gang leader hiding in San Bernardino, and the other man and the girl hiding in Long Beach. They all got put in Los Angeles County Jail, and the trial started a month later. It lasted three months. I took the witness stand once.

Did you make eye contact with the gang members?

One of them was smiling, but the gang leader was looking down. At the time, I was sixty-two years old. His public defender asked me, "If you're the professional boxer, why didn't you fight back?" I said because they surprised me by hitting me in the back of the head and I passed out.*

Did you ever feel like they'd get off and be found not guilty?

Never. Because it was a clear court case, and all those people were already in the system for crimes they'd done. The one got twelve years, but the gang leader got sixteen years and the girl who stepped on my face with her high heels got five. I am very thankful for the American justice

---

* An article in the *Long Beach Press-Telegram* from July 1, 2007, quoted Oum Ry's student Maron May, who saw this response as part of Oum Ry's teachings of non-violence. "The whole idea about being a master is not just fighting and fighting back. [.. It's] about respect, and that shouldn't have happened. Everyone in our community says the same thing, it's outrageous." In a movie, wrote the *Press-Telegram*, "Ban would have fought off his attackers on the Long Beach street, unleashing devastating knees and elbows for which he is renowned. Reality isn't so neatly scripted."

system. Of all the painful things that happened to me over my life, I had never experienced justice before. It was always, just barely escape and don't look back. But the police and the courts did an excellent job.

I found out later that one of them was in the Tiny Rascal Gang and the other was the leader of Azian Boyz. These two gangs had been fighting each other for years, but they agreed on a truce, and decided to beat someone up as a ceremony for their new partnership. I just happened to walk into that restaurant on that night, and they just happened to have drama with my ex. I got very unlucky.

In prison, one of them bragged about hitting me. I had former students in that same jail, and when they found out, they beat him every morning. He begged to move to another jail, and when they transferred him, my former students sent a message to their friends in that jail to punish him.

Did you ever see any of them once they got out?

I never saw them, but I never feared them. Actually, I want to meet them.

If you could meet them today, what would you say?

I wouldn't say anything. I want to see if they'd apologize.

I just felt ashamed because in my whole life, no one ever touched me like that. During Pol Pot, they starved us, but I was never beat like that. Even when Serey Ka tied my hands and threatened to kill me, nobody hit me or anything. When I came to the United States, I thought I was in heaven but then the violence followed me.

I felt sorry for myself because I fought three hundred Pradal Serey matches, and I never got knocked out. I felt embarrassed because Oum Ry the fighter allowed people to hit him.

*Did you ever hear from your ex about what happened
with her and the gang?*

She told the gang that if they wanted to kill her, they can't
because she is with Oum Ry. When she had me around, she
felt powerful and cocky and acted like a queen. She thought
no one could touch her. But then when I got knocked out,
she changed a lot, she became even more mean. She said bad
things about me, like I'm weak. Before, she was attracted to
me when I was powerful, but after the incident, it was like
I was worthless to her.

But on the good side of things, very soon after the attack,
the gangs started fading away. I've had twenty or thirty
people tell me that after they attacked me in November of
2006, the power of the gangs has been reduced dramatically.
These days we still have problems, but they are nothing like
how bad it used to be. I think this is for a lot of reasons — the
main one was that the police got serious about arresting
the leaders of the gangs. And once the two that attacked me
were removed as the leaders, the gangs were weakened.[10]

10

→ Return →

Oum Ry has been fully conked out this last leg of the trip. Seventeen hours from Los Angeles, with an eight-hour layover in Singapore, plus two more hours to Cambodia, has him almost comatose.

As I adjust the pillow behind his head, I think about his stories of surviving the war — all the corpses he buried, endless nights of fear and starvation, the eight months living in the mountains, seeing people explode right in front of him. I try to put myself in thirty-five-year-old Oum Ry's shoes, fleeing the only country he's ever known, not knowing when or if ever he'd go back.

After all the interviews we've done and learning more about what my father (and all Cambodians) went through in the Pol Pot years, I am concerned about what could happen if he sees or hears something that brings on a debilitating

PTSD flashback. I've seen his rage when we are home in Long Beach — if he gets triggered in Cambodia, how will we handle it? Though I am excited for this trip, this is my biggest fear. Looking at my dad passed out on the plane puts me at ease; he's going to need to use whatever energy he has once we land because we don't know what's in store for him.

As if he had an internal alarm in him, Oum Ry opens his eyes just fifteen minutes before we land. We break through the clouds and are met with the vibrant acres of green rice paddies and the Mekong River. He has his arms crossed and mask on, intently staring out the window to soak in the sight of his homeland from more than half a lifetime ago. His eyes subtly widen with interest in front of the view of all the skyscrapers and other modern architecture. Not once does he divert his eyes away from the window until we are on the ground.

When we get off the plane, Oum Ry is so drowsy and jet-lagged that he looks like he is sleepwalking. I put my arm around his shoulder and navigate us through the crowded airport, pushing everyone out of our way, like I am my dad's bodyguard. He simultaneously looks overwhelmed and numb.

While passing through customs, my dad strikes up a conversation with an airport worker. They start talking about Pradal Serey.

"I am actually a former kickboxer myself — I am Oum Ry," my dad mentions.

"Wow! You are Oum Ry?! I've heard stories about you! I didn't know you survived the war! What are you doing here?!"

The man appears to be in his mid-thirties, and my dad is surprised and flattered that someone so young recognizes him. With a soft smile, Oum Ry averts his eyes to the ground for a second, like he usually does when someone compliments him. The worker requests a selfie with my dad, genuinely beaming with happiness. After this interaction, Oum Ry suddenly stops looking tired and walks with his chest out, now invigorated.

We step outside and there it is — the scent of burning wood and fragrant rumduol flower mixed with the physical sensation of the humid, tropical air. This is the smell I associate with Cambodia and wonder if it has always smelled like this?

Waiting outside the airport for us are Racy and her husband, Vichet. Racy is my dad's niece, the daughter of his older brother, Oum Suntoum, who passed away just three months before we arrived. They have spoken on the phone for years, but since she was born after my dad left Cambodia, they have never actually met. Racy has become a successful businesswoman, owning a small hotel and several karaoke bars around Phnom Penh; Vichet works for the federal military of Cambodia.

It is dark out once we leave the airport, and the roads heading to Racy's are extremely dim. For someone who doesn't have twenty-twenty vision and without his glasses, my dad suddenly has perfect sight. He is amazed by how the roads are simply "paved" with paint. He is enthralled by the islands in the streets that divide the roads. Even though I've been to Cambodia several times before, I feel like I am vicariously experiencing everything for the first time with him, just from his priceless reactions. He keeps shaking his head and making that "thsk" sound Cambodians make when we're taken aback. We make this clicking sound with our mouths and usually perk our lips when we're surprised by something.

Every few streets we drive down, he asks Vichet if this street was that street, and most of his questions are met with a no, or that's changed, but none of it bothers my dad. He looks at the buildings with such awe and even claps his hands anytime we see a building taller than two hundred feet.

"They have 7-Eleven here?" He nearly convulses, jerking his head as we drive past his favorite establishment. "I must open a 7-Eleven here and you can be manager, Srey Meas*," he says, calling me by my other given Khmer name. "What do you think?"

I shake my head in amusement, before bursting into laughter.

When a family visits from abroad, staying at a hotel is considered "wasting money" and I may add, disrespectful and offensive. Racy and Vichet have insisted on us staying with them for the duration — she called the entire month off work to facilitate our trip, and he is to be our chauffeur most times, navigating us through the unfamiliar parts of Phnom Penh, a bustling city of two million people.

Tonight, Yeay (grandma) has prepared all the food, as she will every day for our whole month-long stay. Following the customary Cambodian style of eating a meal together, she and Racy bring out the traditional hand-woven mats called kuthale made of straw and bamboo and spread them out on the floor for everyone to sit and feast on.

My dad doesn't request anything special, but the foods from his childhood and the flood of home cooking leave him no choice but to devour everything.

We eat samlor machu srae (sour fish soup), which consists mostly of fish, water spinach, krill, and tamarind, and is considered the household Cambodian soup in the countryside; trei ngeat (dried fish), dehydrated fish that's heavily cured in salt; an array of fresh vegetables that my dad forgot existed and so much fruit; and pahut trei (fish patty/meatball), a traditional fried fish cake that involves pounded fish and fragrant ingredients like lime leaf, lemongrass, and turmeric.

* My name Meas directly translates to "gold," and my nickname growing up was "golden child."

The next morning, our day begins at six-thirty a.m. with another meal, one of the more simple and traditional Cambodian breakfasts: plain rice porridge that's typically eaten with trei ngeat, salted duck egg, and chruok spey (pickled vegetables). Oum Ry ends up having three bowls.

We've been planning this trip for two months, and I have no idea what to expect. The last time he was here, he floated above everything, not being grounded in family and memories. This time will be all about that, about showing me his Cambodia, reliving his youth. Will he still feel a strong connection to Cambodia since so much has changed in the forty-two years since he left? Does he still feel Cambodia is his home? Or will it be unbearable, so much that he will want to go back early?

In the days leading up to our departure, my dad expressed to me what he really hoped for on this trip. He wanted to meet with his first-born son, Oum Pee, who he talks to since the early 2000s and now has connected with on Facebook. They have not been together with in the same room since the Khmer Rouge took over in 1975. He wanted to see his good friend Chhit Sarim, one of the only living Pradal Serey fighters from the pre-war era, and his friend who invited Oum Ry to join the massive convoy headed to Phnom Penh right after the war. He wanted to teach some classes at modern Cambodian gyms to connect with this generation of fighters and see how the art has changed since his days in the ring. And finally, and maybe most importantly to him, my dad tells me he has three girlfriends in Cambodia (he met all three on Facebook) and he plans on meeting each one in person, as often as he can.

I asked him if he wanted to find and meet Pich Dovann, his wife who he lived with for the four years after the Khmer Rouge took over the country. During our interviews, my dad told me he heard she married a wealthy man who works for the government, and that they had two children and lived very comfortable lives. I fully expected he would want to see her, but I was very wrong. He made many excuses why it wouldn't work, none of which made any real sense, but it didn't matter because they were all excuses, and he refused to even discuss it. I can only assume that it was too big of an open wound and could bring back too much pain, more than he could handle at the moment. I wanted so badly to change his mind, but one thing I have learned over the years is that trying to prevail upon a stubborn, nearly seventy-eight-year-old fighter is the definition of a fool's errand, so, I conceded and dropped the subject.

This morning, as we drive through Phnom Penh and play tourists, I watch my dad get excited at things we generally find mundane, and this brings me great joy. We are two sides of the same coin — he is full of pride that his baby girl knows her way around the motherlands, and for me, it's a sweet and strange feeling reintroducing my dad to his homeland.

Since Vichet works for the military, before our arrival he spread the word though government channels that Oum Ry would be returning to visit. Thus, we have been invited twice to meet with government ministers, both of whom were old enough to have seen Oum Ry in the ring in the late sixties and are excited to meet the hero of their childhood.

Today we are invited to the government complex which houses the Ministry of Culture, for a formal meet and greet. My father is genuinely touched by the reception — the minister has surprised him with an impromptu press conference. With several reporters and cameramen, Oum Ry handles the spotlight like a champ.

It is sweet to see my father both being both proud and humbled at the same time.

The following week we are invited to meet the Minister of Sport, who has arranged for us to have VIP seating to watch fifteen Pradal Serey matches live, as they are being televised. There will be more reporters, and he has agreed to be in photos with all the fighters.

Later that night, we meet up with his old fighting friend Chhit Sarim, who was a driver in that huge convoy with goods from Thailand, headed for Phnom Penh. It was on the way back north in the same convoy that the Vietnamese tried to arrest my dad in Siem Reap. They have so much history together, opponents inside the ring and friends outside of it, and it appears at this point that they are the only two champion Pradal Serey fighters still alive from that era.

Chhit Sarim stayed in the fighting world, as both a coach and as a referee for professional fights and just retired a few years ago. He also has a second job as a driver and possesses an impressive zen-like calm as he navigates us through the fluid chaos of the Phnom Penh streets.

The duo got together nearly every day for a few hours, sitting in silence half of the time. Most of their conversations were about the current fighters of Cambodia, their debate on the topic of whether Toyota or Honda was more reliable, and Oum Ry's rather scandalous romantic trysts.

Chhit Sarim was one of the very first people who came to see us. The first morning, I woke up to the sound of my dad howling. *Which one of his girlfriends decided to stop by this early?* I pondered for a few minutes before marching downstairs to the living room, where I saw a man sitting next to my dad on the wooden furniture. My dad's left hand was playfully slapping the man's kneecap as they burst into fits of laughter. "Forty-five years," they repeated to each other in unison, shaking their heads in disbelief. I felt instant goosebumps as I realized who he was. I stayed quiet, not wanting to ruin their moment, tucked away like a child in the corner.

"Ah choi mai!" Chhit Sarim called out my dad — "mother-fucker." It's a vulgar way of joking, but pretty normal among Cambodians. Chhit Sarim is bigger and browner than Oum Ry, and his smile is offset by a gold crown tooth that would shine every time he'd open his mouth.

"I never thought this day would come, my friend," Chhit Sarim was shaking his head so much that his glasses almost fell off.

"I know, my friend. I didn't think I would've made my way here if it weren't for my daughter." They both looked at me in unison as my dad grabbed Chhit Sarim's hand, facing me, shaking it in excitement. For all intents and purposes, in Oum Ry's mind as well as my own, this is his first time back.

On our third day in Cambodia, we set out to reunite with my oldest brother, Oum Pee, the son of my dad's first girl-friend, Khou Kimny, which was his first serious relation-ship as well as the first woman to his knowledge that he got pregnant.

Oum Pee lives in a small town on the banks of the Mekong River called Kampong Chham, about sixty minutes out of Phnom Penh. The further out of the city we get, the more we find unpaved dirt with Aunties (Mings) selling their delicious roadside delicacies of fried cockroaches and taran-tulas, and naked children running around, swimming in the river. But on the whole ride, Oum Ry doesn't speak much, and he looks unusually pensive. I recalled our interview just two months ago when he told me, "When I see Oum Pee, I want to tell him that I love him."

When we pull into the property, seven people surround our car as we get out; mostly men, and no one hugs each other.

"Hi, Pa."

The voice is timid and with so many people around, I can't match the voice to a face. No one is really talking, but they gesture for us to sit down. Now there are at least fifteen people surrounding us as we sit in a circle in silence. To my dad's left is a man who appears to be in his mid-sixties. Could that be my brother? He seems a bit too old to be my dad's son, but they are the only ones engaging in conversation. For the first fifteen minutes that we are there, they talk intently about fighting, both in the distant past and the present. Finally, the man to my dad's right, who hasn't said a word the whole time, suddenly asks with a shy smile, "So, do I look like Dad?"

About five-foot-seven and with a healthy build to him, he has golden brown skin and monolid eyes. Cambodians generally don't have monolid eyes unless they have some Chinese heritage. I don't think he looks like my dad at all, and truthfully, I have not been paying much attention to him. Sometimes I catch him from the corner of my eye staring at me, though he is always quick to look away when we make eye contact.

But this is Oum Pee. My dad's son, who he has been away from since 1975, is now sitting next to him, neither of them really interacting with each other, aside from the very quick eye contact they have before my dad resumes conversation with his friend sitting on his other side. I find this so absurd and confusing. I feel guilty that my dad barely acknowledges him, seeming more interested in his friend than his own son. I turn my attention to Oum Pee, and it dawns on me that he is the most gentle person in the room. He looks at our dad in such awe when speaking, his eyes low and his voice tender. My focus remains on Oum Pee after that, and my dad's on his friends.

Then a woman runs up to my dad, holding a baby in her arms, crying, "Grandpa, I can't believe I am finally meeting you. I never imagined this day would happen."

I am witnessing everything from a few feet away, facing my dad. As she violently sobs into my dad's chest, he nervously looks at me before awkwardly laughing, while stroking her hair. He is looking mostly at me though, like he is communicating with me through his eyes.

"This is your great-granddaughter, tha*."

She has my dad hold her baby, while she attempts to wipe her tears away but continues crying. At this moment, I felt such annoyance at my dad, but also sympathy for him. Why didn't he hold her tight as she sobbed into his arms? Why didn't he acknowledge his son? Why did he mostly look at me instead of her? I had so many questions for which I knew I wouldn't get an answer. He just met his fifty-six-year-old son, met eight grandkids and an additional eleven great-grandkids, and he was acting like it was just a regular day in the office. I have to respect the way my dad was processing all of this overwhelming information, but I still find it baffling.

It makes a little more sense once we are all in the car on the way back to Phnom Penh. Oum Ry is even more quiet than on the drive earlier today.

"I'm sad," he says. I squeeze his hand as he slowly puts his thoughts together. "I'm sad that my family is poor. I cannot do much because I am poor too."

While connecting with Chhit Sarim and Oum Pee has been good for my father's heart, he is not hiding the fact that something else even more pressing is on his mind. On our first night in Cambodia, Oum Ry announced to the family that he had three girlfriends in Cambodia, that he met all of them three years ago on Facebook, and that he wanted to spend as much time with them as he could.

My father has always been the consummate player. I

* "Tha" means "grandpa" in Khmer.

remember when I was eleven years old overhearing him telling a friend that he has had sex with over a thousand women during his fifteen-year fighting career. I know it wasn't just fantasy conquest talk either — he was the top athlete and one of the most famous people in his country, always spent all his money, and in his heyday he was extremely fit and handsome. Even when he came to Long Beach, his legend followed him, and women would go to great lengths to be introduced to the champion Oum Ry.

So now, at the age of seventy-seven and returning to the land of his former glory, Oum Ry is determined to meet his three girlfriends. Of course, being who I am, I instinctively want to protect my father. Why would a thirty-three-year-old woman be "dating" a man forty-four years older than her unless she is scheming to get something? Is one of the reasons he is always broke back home because he is wiring money to his women? Am I going to have a new stepmom soon? I do not mention this to my father, fearing a meltdown. I just watch from the sidelines, doing my best not to get involved or even have too much judgment.

"My second girlfriend might be too 'old' for me, she is forty-two years old," he jokes. "So many women still want me! But they are trouble."

—◆◇◆—

"It's been four days since I last trained, and I feel fat," my dad confides to me as we make our way to the first workshop class at Kingdom Fight Gym in Phnom Penh. Oum Ry hasn't done any preparation, nor does he have anything planned. I guess he is going to improvise once we get there.

We are respectfully greeted by seven trainers from the gym, and my dad quickly connects with the young Khmer fighters. The owner, a Chinese-Dutch man named Kwok, is kind enough to give my dad Kun Khmer shorts, which he puts on immediately. I haven't seen my dad wear Khmer kickboxing shorts since I was a little girl, and it brought me joy seeing him bounce around in traditional attire.

He starts off the class by explaining his backstory, then talking about how he ended up back in Cambodia. All seven of the trainers attending the workshop are also professional fighters, so my dad decides to teach them more advanced and technical moves.

We start off with ten minutes of stretching, followed by fifteen minutes of jumping rope. Oum Ry says jumping rope is a crucial part of training because it builds stamina and helps with your footwork. He has them shadow box in the mirror for fifteen minutes; it helps embed technique in your muscle memory. Oum Ry has the seven men line up side by side as they face him, where he breaks down the technicalities of his favorite moves and how to deliberately execute them.

"Khmer fighters must train more with their hands. Westerners are better at boxing than us. We also need to work on better defense," he tells them, and they all agree.

My dad demonstrates these techniques on one of the fighters, and everyone is unbelievably wowed by how fast and strong a seventy-seven-year-old man can be. I mean, I see my dad train almost every day, and I'm still utterly impressed by his strength and agility. A part of the technique is to make your opponent fall to the floor, and Oum Ry effortlessly brings the young fighter to the ground in the blink of an eye — as the young Khmer fighter throws a right high kick at Oum Ry, my dad sweeps the fighter with a low left inside kick, causing him to fall over.

The second move they're going over is one of my dad's ultimate favorites because it requires elbows, which were his specialty. When your opponent throws a roundhouse, you'd catch their leg with one arm, and with the opposite arm you throw a dagger-like elbow to the inside of their thigh, then followed by a spinning back elbow to their face.

Over the next hour and a half, he has everyone partner up and perform the technique on each other.

The students are well pleased with the lessons they absorbed today, and my dad is proud to pass the knowledge down to the young Khmer fighters. After class is over, we all decide to have a celebratory meal where Oum Ry is beaming with joy.

Two weeks after the successful workshop at Kingdom Fight Gym in Phnom Penh, we make our way to their second location in Siem Reap. This location is much bigger than the other one in Phnom Penh and has more of a 'primitive' style to it; the roof is a metal triangle and the sides are exposed so it has a lot of natural lightning and air flowing through. Another Pradal Serey group from Mr Ly Gym & Boxing is waiting for us and joins in on the workshop. On the drive over to the gym, he was anxious about the class not having a big turnout. "What if no one attends the class? What if no one remembers who I am?" I imagine these doubts replaying constantly in his head as we walk into the gym, head low, until his gaze is met with over two dozen students lined up to meet him. Everyone has their hands behind their back until they bow to my dad, or *sampeah* which is a Cambodian way of showing respect. Oum Ry has to do a double take because he is in disbelief. Humbled and overwhelmed, he profusely expresses his gratitude to everyone, one by one.

My dad performs his usual schtick before breaking down the moves for the class to perform on each other. He'll explain his backstory of how and why he started with Pradal Serey, before someone in the class will comment about his promiscuously debauched days, causing Oum Ry to turn red. Getting distracted by that comment, he will go on a tangent about his heydays with the ladies before completing his story.

Oum Ry demonstrates the same few techniques for the other gym with one of the head trainers in front of the class before he has everyone practice with one another. Most of the students are professional fighters, and a few of them are still trying to break into the fight world.

The liveliness of the gym is rejuvenating my dad's energy as he faces nearly two dozen students, going over techniques and goofing around with the fighters. Intensely sweating as he bounces around, my dad is panting for air in between laughs. I haven't seen him this animated while training students in a very long time, and it reminds me of how he'd train his students when I was young. As he finishes, jokingly sparring with the young Khmer fighter, Oum Ry takes a breather and everyone in the gym cheers for him.

After the success of his Siem Reap workshop, my dad is finally able to relax. Though he doesn't want to admit it; he puts a lot of pressure on himself to live up to his legacy, but the large turnout of enthusiastic fighters has lifted his spirits.

The plans are to wake up the next morning at five a.m. to go see the sunrise at Angkor Wat. The ancient temples, built in the eighth through eleventh centuries, with seventy-two structures covering over four hundred acres, are to this day the largest religious complex in the world. Not only is the size of it mind boggling, but the detail and beauty of the stone carvings on the temple walls are so intricate that it had to be made by artisans and not slaves. It is unlike anything else in the world, and is the pride of every Cambodian, at home and abroad.

I was expecting my dad to join me, but instead Oum Ry says he will also wake up at five a.m., but in order to watch the

Super Bowl live on television. How can he pass up seeing his ancestors' most profound contribution to humanity in order to watch yet another manufactured sporting spectacle? Part of me finds it incomprehensible, but I remember that he has lived in America more than half his life, and there is a kind of sweetness in how he has reinvented himself with American customs.

Since we are the first wave of people to visit Siem Reap after the Covid restrictions have been lifted, the temples are almost empty. My tuk tuk (auto rickshaw) drops me off at the main temple at five-thirty a.m., while everything is still dark. Sunrise is not dramatic, but instead the gentle haze slowly illuminates the massive temple structure. It seems to emerge out of a dark gray fog and hover in the humid jungle air. At seven-thirty a.m. I take another tuk tuk to the Ta Prohm temple, which has been completely swallowed up by the jungle and lies in a semi-ruined state. Towering trees, at least fifty-feet tall, have grown on top of the temple, with muscular roots spilling over the ramparts like the tentacles of a gigantic octopus. I've never seen trees like this before — even the bark seems to be painted a metallic gold. I sit alone in Ta Prohm for over an hour, bonding with a giant tree, ancient yet alive, and am overwhelmed with the beauty of impermanence, that this temple is so big and strong to have survived over a thousand years in the harsh jungle weather, yet for most of those thousand years it has been completely forgotten to people, and that trees growing out of it, reclaiming it, prove the endless rebirth of nature. It is almost as if the tree is telling me that as scary as the ephemeral nature of life is, as much as it hurts to say goodbye to those we love, there is beauty in trying to make the most of our short time here.

I am so blissed out that I am neither surprised nor irritated when my dad and family are almost three hours late. I am just happy to share this experience with Oum Ry. From the late sixties to the mid-seventies, he had come to Siem

Reap several times for fights — but he never actually took the time to visit the temples. He says that he only thought about fighting (and chasing women, I might add), and that he just didn't have time for field trips.

I don't think he really knows what to expect and within minutes of getting close to the temple, he starts to visibly transform. Usually social and chatting with everyone around him, he becomes more introverted and pensive. He and I break off from the family and wander around together, not speaking, but in a constant state of wonder and awe at the scale, the age, the detail, and the endurance of the temples.

Then, as if the rest of the world doesn't exist, my father starts praying to Ta Kaan, directly talking with his guardian spirit as if it is standing right in front of him. His voice is muted, but he is speaking quickly — I can make out the word Ta Kaan, but little else. But somehow a light has turned on inside of him and he understands the importance of this place, and his connection to it. I give him some space, and he continues walking and talking like this for at least ten minutes.

Later that night, I asked Oum Ry what he was saying to Ta Kaan.

"Ta Kaan said it was finally time for my arrival back and that I must keep going." I can feel the lump in my throat start to form as he finishes that last part.

"Ta Kaan seems to never be wrong. Is that all he said?" I respond back with glossy eyes.

"I told him to watch over the family and you. He must bring you good luck and protection."

Three or four days before our return flight to California, Oum Ry is invited to dinner by a wealthy Cambodian businessman who remembered seeing a fight in the early 1970s. We take a tuk tuk about fifteen minutes out of town and arrive at the Tonle Sap River, where our host owns a house-boat. We will dine on the water.

We arrive ten minutes early and use the opportunity to take some low-key dramatic portraits of each other standing in front of the river with the sun setting on the city. Finally, our host arrives, carrying a bottle of scotch and a bucket of ice. His red face and bombastic volume hints at the fact that he has been working on that bottle already for quite a while.

During dinner (grilled duck, banana lotus leaf salad with shrimp and pork, fried fish and rice) our host insists on distributing refills of booze, so there is always something new to toast about.

The dinner conversation consists of the regular topics that men of that age discuss — old memories from before the war, reminiscing about Oum Ry's fights at the Olympic Stadium, and the quality of today's Pradal Serey fighters. But in the middle of the dinner, I hear my father say something, almost offhandedly, that startles me.

"Before I came back here, I didn't know who I was. But now I know who I am. I am Oum Ry."

In the tuk tuk ride back to Racy's house, I ask my dad what he meant by that. "They tried to kill me so many times," he says, "but I am still alive. Cambodia was the only home I knew. When I left, I had to start my life all over again. I had never been to a Western country, I spoke no English, I had never even seen snow. I made a new life in America. And now that I am back, I feel like my life in Cambodia and my life in America are one."

—◆○◆—

Fighting was and still is a means of survival for Oum Ry. The life of a fighter is mentally and physically draining with low rewards. To succeed you need an almost super-human level of dedication, sacrifice and endurance, yet few are champions, and most carry their injuries for the rest of their lives. It's in my father's blood, and I used to think it was in my blood too, but I now realize I have a more complex relationship with it.

After I turned eighteen, I felt constant pressure from those around us for me to take over my dad's gym. I've trained there ever since I was a small child — I literally took my first steps inside that ring. It's only natural for me to want to fill my dad's gloves. But Oum Ry never allowed me to compete, saying that he fought because he needed the money, that I live in America, and I have so many other opportunities. And because I would never want to fight without my father as my cornerman, and since he would never agree to do it, it has left us in a confusing and unsettled space. At times, my dad would tell me he doesn't want me to pursue this lifestyle and instead, to go to school and have a career. Other times, he'd push me so hard during training until I cried because, according to him, I "have no choice but to take over the gym" when he's gone. This is still an open question as I teach classes and help train the fighters, and I'm still trying to figure out what the answer will be.

—◆○◆—

As our flight home approaches, Oum Ry is looking forward to going back to Long Beach and making sure everything at the gym is going smoothly. Our last few days in Cambodia are spent running around Phnom Penh and doing chores, mostly collecting an absurd amount of trei ngeat (dried fish), prahok (fermented fish paste), and other potent smelling items to bring back for some Long Beach Cambodians to eat and sell — three suitcases and two boxes in all. I'll spare you the gory details, but it involved a lot of yelling and swearing over the phone, as these particular people can be demanding and ruthless when it comes to smelly food and making money.

The morning we leave, I wake up at five a.m. and finish my packing. As I tape up the last box, I take a moment to reflect on the fact that my father didn't have the debilitating PTSD flashback I was so concerned about as we flew over here. I am both surprised and incredibly grateful. In fact, the opposite seems to be the case. The friends, the family, and all the fans asking for selfies have rejuvenated his spirit. He has even started talking about coming back in the coming years with a couple fighters whom he trains so that they can compete against both Cambodians and Thais.

On the ride to the airport, my father and I both stare out the windows, silently, taking in our last impressions of the colonial architecture from French occupation, the street signs, and the beehive of scooters and trucks. I glance over at him, and I think about the time that fourteen-year-old Oum Ry saw the men practicing Pradal Serey for the first time, and instantly, intuitively, felt he could become a champion. I think about the thousands of people at the Olympic Stadium who roared for their favorite fighter, he with the smallest frame and the biggest heart. I think about how the Khmer Rouge made a point of killing all the celebrities in Cambodia, and how my father was one of the only famous people to escape the slaughter and starvation. I think about how he started one of the very first kickboxing gyms in the United States, and how it has been open six days a week for thirty-five years.

"Bye, big brother — I will see you soon, okay?" We are video chatting with Oum Pee as we sit at our terminal in the airport.

"Please don't forget me," he says to us. "I feel my life is complete now that I have my father and my little sister. I am complete." He isn't looking directly at the camera, and I find it almost impossible to keep myself composed — my throat tightens and I clench my jaws, knowing that if I start crying I won't be able to stop.

I turn the phone over to my dad, resting my head on his shoulder, so he can talk with my brother. It feels comforting calling him my brother. It feels right. "I will call you when we land, kuon. Pa sralang kuon*." My dad is smiling and sniff-kissing me on the forehead. My brother's eyes are visibly red. He clears his throat.

"I love you too, dad. I love you both. Have a safe flight home."

* In Khmer, people refer to each other in the third person. This translates into "Pa loves son."

⟿⟿ Notes ⟿⟿

1 The city of Long Beach, California has the largest population of Cambodians living abroad. This is largely due to California State University Long Beach. In the 1950s and 1960s, the Cambodian and the American governments created a program for Cambodian students to attend California colleges and universities. The students studied practical skills — agriculture, industrial arts, and engineering — with the idea that after completing their degrees, the students would return home to contribute their skills in Cambodian society. However, several students decided to remain in the United States permanently. After the end of the Pol Pot regime, the first waves of Cambodian refugees came to the United States through Camp Pendleton, which is thirty-five miles south of Long Beach. The former students brought them meals and supplies; they ended up sponsoring refugees to earn their citizenship and to help them adjust to life in a foreign country. This student support system resulted in the formation of the Cambodian Association of America, which attracted subsequent refugees who came to Long Beach. Today, roughly twenty thousand Cambodians, or people of Cambodian descent, live in Long Beach, making up four percent of the population.

2 The official number of Covid deaths reported worldwide, six million by May 2022, is clearly an undercount. Many countries haven't reported their official statistics, or those are hidden under the guise of other deaths like "pneumonia" and "heart failure" for people who tested positive or could not be tested at all. Another clear indicator is the number of excess deaths seen in 2020 and 2021 in many countries across the world, leading health agencies to conclude that as of Spring 2022, the number of Covid deaths worldwide is closer to fifteen million.

See Mueller, Benjamin and Stephanie Nolen. "Death Toll During Pandemic Far Exceeds Totals Reported by Countries, W.H.O. Says." *New York Times*. May 5, 2022. https://www.nytimes.com/2022/05/05/health/covid-global-deaths.html

For a graphic count updated frequently, see "Tracking Excess Covid-19 Deaths Across Countries." *The Economist*. No date. https://www.economist.com/graphic-detail/coronavirus-excess-deaths-tracker

3 Palm leaf scrolls are an ancient method used to inscribe religious scriptures, dating all the way back to the fifth century BCE in India, China and Southeast Asia. The palm leaf scrolls are similar to scrolls out of papyrus made by the ancient Egyptians and Greeks centuries before the creation of paper and pen as we know it. The process began by cooking the palm leaves, and it would take roughly a month to process the leaves so they were dry and hard enough to write on. Then they were cut into rectangles, typically had a hole through which a string could pass to bind the sheets together as a kind of book. Writing was done with a stylus, a specially sharpened piece of wood, and later steel, and the writer would carve into the palm leaf scroll. Ink was made from combining fine dust made from charcoal with an alluvial resin, and then the mixture was heated until a black resinous oil was produced. This was rubbed over the manuscript pages with a cloth so that the whole page was covered with black. Then the ink would be rubbed away with sifted rice bran, leaving the black resin in the scratched stylus depressions on the page.

In Cambodia, the palm leaf scrolls were made for inscribing the ancient sacred Buddhist scriptures called "Tripitaka." A palm leaf text would typically last between a few decades to about six hundred years before it decayed due to dampness, insect activity, mold and fragility. One of the oldest surviving palm leaf manuscripts from the ninth century, discovered in Nepal, is now preserved at the Cambridge University Library.

4 After Cambodia claimed independence from France in 1953, King Sihanouk changed the trajectory of the country by modernizing and shaping Phnom Penh into a metropolis for music and social life. This period before the genocide was known as the Golden Era, and Phnom Penh was regarded as The Pearl of Southeast Asia. The city experienced a period of peace and prosperity which was heavily moved by King Sihanouk's political strategies for neutrality and his love for music. King Sihanouk worked to develop urban centers, create an elite class and increase industrialization within the country. Music became a unifying aspect within the 1960s and '70s as Cambodia took musical influence from around the world. Khmer music before the 1960s reflected elements from Afro-Cuban roots, bossa nova, and jazz styles but, with the landing of the U.S. troops in Vietnam, western music and American culture pushed Cambodia into the rock and roll era.

As Phnom Penh became a hub for modernity and encap-
sulated several different musical styles, musicians and
actors such as Sinn Sisamouth and Kong Som Eun grew in
popularity and status. Sinn Sisamouth was born in Stung
Treng Province and became classically trained at the Royal
Palace. With his training, he was able to teach himself com-
position in the western solfege style and produced music
that covered several genres and themes. He quickly adapted
to the rapidly changing music scene and flourished in the
rock and roll era. He was incredibly acclaimed and wrote
over a thousand songs during his ten-year musical career.
Unfortunately, his career came to an end when the Khmer
Rouge took power, and he was killed. His legacy lives on
today as he is still known as the King of Khmer music and
wildly beloved.

Kong Som Eun was born in 1947 and died in 1976; he was most
active during 1964–1975. He was an actor and a film director
and starred in more than half of the films released between
1967–75, with one hundred and twenty films. Some of his
most famous films were *Sovannahong* and *Tep Sodachan*
which are still sold to this day. Although Cambodia went
through a period of artistic and social development, this
claim of a golden era did not reflect the political reality of the
nation. The Khmer Rouge utilized this period of progressive
art to serve their politics by producing nationalistic songs to
instigate a sense of power and suppress any artistic volition
that took away from their political aim. Most recordings
from musicians of this time have been destroyed or are
incredibly rare; when Khmer people look back at this
moment in time, their memory is plagued by the Khmer
Rouge's overtaking of not only the nation but the destruction of the artistic freedom and unification that took place
right before the Khmer Rouge's control.

5 See the Afterword for further information about American
involvement in these historical events.

6 The Preah Vihear Temple was constructed over the course of three hundred years by various kings, including King Yasovarman I, King Suryavarman I and King Suryavarman II. It is an extraordinary Khmer architectural temple originally made to be a Hindu temple for Shiva, but in the twelfth century, it was named a Buddhist monastery. It is known for its location which is on a cliff in the Dangrek Mountains and sits on the border of Thailand and Cambodia. The temple was built on a north-south axis and overlooks the Cambodian plain. It was a center for both communities to enjoy the temple for religious purposes, trade, and a meeting ground for high and low Khmer communities. The location has caused many wars between the bordering countries as Cambodia and Thailand both view the site as a symbol of their national identity. Tensions over the monument started in the beginning of the twentieth century when a map of the border was drawn and the temple was placed in Cambodia even though the marker for the borders was the natural watershed, which fell on Thailand's side, and the new map indicated the temple to be in Thailand's domain. By the time Thailand noticed this mistake, the courts ruled they waited too long and awarded Cambodia dominion. This did not stop the disputes, and the border crossing was closed until November 2013 when the International Court of Justice in the Hague declared that the promontory of Preah Vihear was awarded to Cambodia and Thailand had to withdraw any soldiers from the site.

7 A 2007 report by the U.N. Refugee Agency titled "The Bunong: The Caretakers of Cambodia's Sacred Forests" details the cultural, spiritual and economic life of the remote tribe Oum Ry met in his time on the mountain. Roughly ninety percent of Cambodians are Khmer, and it is estimated that Cambodia's indigenous people comprise about one percent of the country's total population. Of that one percent, a little over half are Bunong.

The Bunong are a two-thousand-year-old tribe of subsistence farmers living in small village communities in forests in the northeast. Traditionally, everything the Bunong need to survive comes from the forest and small hillside fields near their villages, where they farm mangos, bananas, sweet potatoes, pineapple, cassava, eggplant, chilis, and jackfruit, as well as some tobacco and cotton.

Most Bunong, like other hill tribe communities of Southeast Asia, practice animism, the belief in spiritual beings in the forest capable of helping or harming human interests, as well as ancestor worship. As explained by an elder, the Bunong believe that "nature is populated by spirits, both good and bad, and that these must be obeyed and appeased. No spirits are more powerful than those of the Spirit Forests."

It is a belief system based on respect — the Bunong realize that a healthy forest is essential to their cultural survival. They believe that the forest belongs to the spirits, and that everyone should have access to it, so the Bunong do not consider land as a commodity. According to the report, "This egalitarian attitude makes them vulnerable to land theft, a common problem in Cambodia."

The existence and culture of the Bunong is generally ignored. There is little to nothing written about them in school textbooks and the average citizen on the streets of Phnom Penh most likely have never heard of them, yet they have been living by the same values and traditions for centuries before the foundation of the modern state of Cambodia.

8 See the Afterword for more on the details of Thai and Vietnamese involvement in Cambodian politics and borders.

9 The East Side Longos and 18th Street Gang, both primarily Hispanic, ran Long Beach before the introduction of

Southeast Asian gangs. The animosity between Hispanic and Cambodian gangs started in October 1989 when members of the Tiny Rascals gang shot and killed a sixteen-year-old boy named Oswaldo Carbajal, who was part of the East Side Longos. This ethnic war lasted several years, and other gangs began to align themselves with the two sides. Many lives were lost in this dispute as each new casualty resulted in reprisals and an ongoing battle for revenge and power. Between 1989 and 1995, gang wars erupted all over Los Angeles County, with as many as fifty-three gang-related killings and three hundred and forty-one shootings in one year. Many of these shootings were attributed to the ongoing war between Latino and Southeast Asian gangs.

10 As this book is published, our region is dealing with a sudden increase in gun violence and gang-related killings. The city of Los Angeles saw, according to the *Los Angeles Times*, "nearly 400 killings at the end of 2021, a staggering loss of progress in reducing such violence over the last 15 years. As of Dec. 29, 2021 there had been 392 homicides — the most of any year since 2007." The demographics among the dead are very skewed, consisting overwhelmingly of Latino and Black youths and young men. And the same neighborhoods that most suffered in the gang wars of the 1990s are being hard hit again, though upticks are being seen in other areas of the city and county as well.

Rector, Kevin. "Gun violence hits 15-year high in L.A., taking lives and erasing hard-fought gains." *Los Angeles Times*. December 31, 2021. https://www.latimes.com/california/story/2021-12-31/gun-violence-los-angles-15-year-high

⟿∘← Afterword ←∘⟿

"Oum Ry's Life in the Context of Cambodia's History"
by Michael G. Vann, Ph.D.

H istorical context is essential for understanding the twists of fate that shaped the life of Oum Ry, Pradal Serey champion. While many Westerners know generally about Cambodia, and some are familiar with the horrors of the Khmer Rouge's so-called "Killing Fields," an overview of Khmer history can help us make sense of his story.

While Oum Ry emigrated from Cambodia and started a new life in the United States, the country was unstable for decades. Today, Cambodia might be considered a rather small and impoverished nation-state in an isolated corner of Southeast Asia. However, a thousand years ago it was the center of one of the world's great empires. With landholdings larger than its European contemporary, the Byzantine

Empire, at its height, the Khmer Empire (802–1431) covered most of what today is Cambodia, Thailand, Laos, and southern Vietnam, as well as claiming suzerainty over parts of Myanmar and Malaysia. Its capital city, Yaśodharapura (more commonly referred to as Angkor), may have been home to as many as one million inhabitants. Visitors favorably commented upon its size, wealth, and orderliness. Surviving structures such as Angkor Wat's towers and kilometers of galleries, the imposing city walls of Angkor Thom, and the intricate carvings of the Bayon and Banteay Srei temples impressed medieval religious pilgrims as much as they do twenty-first century tourists. Archeologists are still discovering evidence of the massive size and technological sophistication of Khmer urban centers. Angkor Wat remains the world's largest religious complex.

The legacy of the Khmer Empire is a point of nationalist pride for many contemporary Cambodians.

The Khmer Empire owed its success to a combination of geography and statecraft. There were various kingdoms that preceded the empire. Chinese sources referred to Funan, a region of loosely aligned states around the lower Mekong River from the first to seventh centuries of the Common Era. Later records refer to Chenla as a possibly centralized kingdom that governed the Mekong Basin. In 802, a Khmer prince stood atop Mount Mahendraparvata (now known as Phnom Kulen) and declared the region independent and unified. Taking the name Jayavarman II, he reigned for close to five decades and his empire survived him by nearly six centuries. However, after its fifteenth-century collapse, the once powerful empire all but disappeared from the historical record.

While we have relatively few written sources from the era, scholars have established some key elements of Khmer rule. First, the Khmer Empire followed the Mandala model, a common political pattern in pre-modern Southeast Asia.

Mandala states had central capitals where a royal family in a palace exercised complete power but as one moved further from the center, the monarch's control became less absolute. The boundaries between states were often grey zones where two or more kings might compete for influence. While the flexibility of the Mandala era's borders could avoid conflict between early modern kingdoms, in the nineteenth and twentieth centuries, the vague frontiers between Cambodia and Thailand to the west and Vietnam to the east led to serious tensions and a series of wars. Second, the Khmer empire adopted the Indian Devaraja system, in which the monarch was a "god-king." As an embodiment or avatar of Hindu deities such as Shiva or Vishnu, the king's body was a source of spiritual as well as political power. Aspects of this tradition have survived into the modern era with both Cambodian and Thai kings commanding wide ranging authority and secular political leaders using similar forms of charismatic authority.

Centuries of contact with South Asia brought in numerous Indian influences. Both merchants and Brahmin holy men came to present-day Cambodia. An older school of Western scholarship referred to the Khmer Empire as an "Indianized state." The Khmer Empire was initially Hindu with a Mahayana Buddhist minority. Scenes from the *Ramayana* and the *Mahabharata* decorated royal palaces and sacred sites. As elsewhere in Southeast Asia, these two Hindu epics dominate Khmer performing arts which include both dance and shadow puppetry. However, after the thirteenth century, Theravada Buddhism from Sri Lanka (with its arguably more populist message) won over many converts. Regardless, Buddhism did not displace Hindu traditions but rather blended with them. Animism dominated village culture. To this day, sacred sites, local spirits and deities, and respected holy figures inform many Cambodians' worldview. We can see this in Oum Ry's respect for Yeay Puch's prophesies and his prayers to Ta Kaan.

In addition to spectacular temples and palaces, the rulers of Angkor built roads, canals, and massive reservoirs known as baray. These baray collected water from local downpours and flooding rivers in the May to October monsoon season, allowing for crops to be irrigated during the dry months. With the state building and maintaining this hydraulic infrastructure, the kings ensured that their subjects could grow multiple rice crops per year. Combined with the rich alluvial soil of the Mekong Basin, the plentiful fisheries of the Tonle Sap Lake, and the rich forests of the relatively low mountain ranges, the empire was an economic powerhouse. It was also well situated to participate in regional trade as well as commerce between India and China. Thus, the Khmer emperor presided over a massive tax base. This wealth funded gigantic construction projects as well as large standing armies. The Bayon, a Buddhist temple built by Jayavarman VII, contains detailed depictions of his army and Chinese mercenaries defeating Cham invaders between 1178 and 1181. The Bayon also shows his soldiers training for combat. These are some of the earliest images of Pradal Serey or Khmer kickboxing (see photo, page 172).

While Jayavarman VII defeated the Muslim Cham invaders from what is now coastal Vietnam, his successors faced a more serious threats from the lands to the west. In the fourteenth century, Angkor had trouble controlling the peripheral lands, and local lords challenged Khmer authority. In the 1350s, 1393, and 1431, the Siamese Kingdom of Ayutthaya (1351–1767) invaded the center of the Khmer Mandala. A devastating seven-month siege and subsequent sacking of the capital spelled the end of the Khmer Empire. Ironically, Ayutthaya adopted numerous aspects of Khmer statecraft, architecture, and other cultural forms into what would become modern Thailand. This can be seen in the Thai dominance of Southeast Asian martial arts. Many fight fans think "Muay Thai" is synonym for "kickboxing" and have never heard of its Cambodian origins as Pradal Serey.

Today it is a huge faux pas to refer to the various forms of Khmer kickboxing as "Muay Thai" (I learned this the hard way from a Phnom Penh taxi driver who was fiercely proud of his nation's traditions).

While the Khmer kings fled their once great capital on the Tonle Sap, they reestablished themselves on the banks of the Mekong. Phnom Penh served as a capital from 1432 to 1505. Sitting at the confluence of four rivers, the city was a significant market center for centuries. A range of foreign merchants, including Japanese and Portuguese, settled there, but Chinese increasingly dominated the city's commerce. In these centuries, Cambodia lost much of its previous social complexity and entered a period some historians refer to as a Dark Age. Scholars are currently trying to understand Khmer decline, but it appears that environmental factors and socio-political changes combined to weaken the once great empire. While never completely abandoned and a destination for regional pilgrims, most of the Angkorian temples and palaces fell into serious neglect. Meanwhile, the rising Siamese and Vietnamese kingdoms annexed Khmer territory. Siamese occupied western Cambodia, including Siem Reap and the Angkorian complex. Vietnamese settlers from the north began to farm in the agriculturally rich Mekong Delta, an area that was not formally brought under Vietnamese control in the 1700s and is still home to many Khmer to this day. Some Vietnamese moved up the Mekong towards Phnom Penh and other trade centers. To make matters worse, the Siamese and Vietnamese fought a series of wars in the eighteenth and nineteenth century in what is today Cambodia, illustrating the proverb "when elephants fight, it is the ants who suffer." In times of peace, the kingdom's powerful neighbors intervened in palace politics and used dynastic succession as a proxy war. In 1834, Emperor Minh Manh formally declared most of present-day Cambodia to be a Vietnamese province known as Tay Thanh. A Khmer rebellion failed in 1840, but a final

Siamese-Vietnamese war led to an independent Cambodia in 1847. Resentment of Siamese and Vietnamese intrusions would influence Khmer nationalism in the twentieth century as seen when Oum Ry remarked that he was happy to be drafted into Lon Nol's army as he wanted to protect Cambodia from Vietnam.

In 1866, King Norodom I (1860–1904) reestablished Phnom Penh as a capital. He was supported in this move by the newly arrived French. Having seized the mouth of the Mekong, the colonizers were eager to see if the river could provide a backdoor to China. To secure access to the river, they pressured Norodom into accepting a "protectorate" over his territory. It is unclear what the Khmer king understood about the French aims, but he was eager to gain a powerful ally against the Siamese monarchy. Unfortunately for the French imperialist adventurers, the Mekong quickly proved to be unfit for navigation (something the locals could have told them). As French energies turned towards northern and southern Vietnam, "Cambodge," as the French called it, became a colonial backwater. While Phnom Penh was home to some truly gorgeous colonial architecture and developed a charm that led it to being called the "Pearl of Asia," the French invested little capital in the rest of the country. Despite the unashamedly self-congratulatory imperialist rhetoric of France's "civilizing mission," the colonial state spent little on schools. Needing a class of civil servants to administer the protectorate, educated Vietnamese moved to Cambodge and occupied some of the best white-collar jobs. This only increased Khmer resentment of their eastern neighbors.

In 1907, France pressured the Thai monarchy to retrocede three western provinces, including the Angkorian complex north of Siem Reap. French colonial archeologists spent considerable time and money studying and rebuilding the Khmer ruins. Fearing Thai influence in their colony,

French scholars tried to establish a specifically Khmer style of Buddhism. Through anthropological and archeological research, colonial authorities sought to define what was Khmer and what was not. This was part of a political strategy to prevent anti-colonial alliances by drawing a clear line on the map between the Kingdom of Siam and the Protectorate of Cambodge, underlining France's claims of protecting Cambodians from supposedly expansionist Thais. While Cambodia's mostly rural population was oblivious to discussions of Khmer identity and Cambodian history, those privileged enough to attend French schools in Phnom Penh did encounter such ideas. Ironically, this imperial strategy of divide and rule laid the seeds for the modern Khmer nationalism that would explode in the late twentieth century.

Another unintended consequence of colonial policies was France's inadvertent introduction of Marxism. In the 1950s, the French offered scholarships for a handful elite students to study in France. While guided towards practical subjects that would be useful in governing a post-colonial Cambodia, these students encountered a range of philosophical and political ideas in post-war Paris. One of the most famous students was Vann Molyvann who initially studied law but transferred to the École Nationale Supérieure des Beaux-Arts and became Cambodia's first certified architect. He would blend Modernism with local design elements to give Phnom Penh a distinctive architectural style in the 1960s known as the New Khmer Architecture. When Oum Ry reminisces about the beauty of Phnom Penh in the late 1960s, he is referring to many of Vann Molyvann's buildings.

Other young Khmer students encountered post-war Paris' radical politics. Marxism was particularly fashionable at the time. Khieu Samphan was a promising economics student who earned his doctorate at the Sorbonne by theorizing an independent and self-reliant Cambodia. Hou Yuon was another brilliant Sorbonne doctorate whose dissertation, *The Cambodian Peasants and Their Prospects for Modernization*, argued that urbanization and industrialization were not necessary for developing rural Cambodia. Two students, Ieng Sary and Khieu Thirith, married in Paris. The bride was studying Shakespeare and was the first Khmer to earn a degree in English literature. Another Cambodian student was Saloth Sar, who was in Paris from 1949 to 1953 to study radio-frequency engineering. A poor student who never felt comfortable in France, he joined other Khmer students in an underground Marxist reading group and joined the French Communist Party (PCF). At the time, the party was one of the largest in France. While party members ran for elections and drew roughly twenty-five percent of the popular vote, the staunch Stalinist Maurice Thorez ran the PCF with a firm hand.

Saloth Sar had difficulty understanding Marx's theoretical details, but he learned the value of Thorez's strict discipline. He was also inspired by Mao Zedong's surprising success in the Chinese Civil War and the possibilities of adapting Marxism to the material conditions of rural Asia. When he returned to Cambodia in 1953, he joined the local Communist movement and became the General Secretary of the Khmer Rouge in the 1960s. By that time, he went by the nom de guerre Pol Pot. Fellow students from Paris including Khieu Samphan, Ieng Sary, Khieu Ponnary (Pol Pot's first wife), Ieng Thirith, Hu Nim, Hou Yuon, and Son Sen would form the core of the leadership of the Khmer Rouge.

Meanwhile, the French colonial empire was starting to crumble. By 1953, France was exhausted from the First Indochina War (1946–1954), an expensive war against Vietnamese freedom fighters. The French agreed to let the young King Norodom Sihanouk declare independence. Within a year, Ho Chi Minh's Vietminh, a Vietnamese Communist dominated coalition, dealt France a devastating defeat at Dien Bien Phu. As France pulled out of Vietnam, there was an agreement to temporarily divide the country between a Communist north and an anti-Communist south until elections could be held by 1956. However, the United States encouraged the new South Vietnamese leader Ngo Dinh Diem to postpone elections as intelligence assessments agreed that Ho Chi Minh's new regime would win the entire nation. Frustrated with the political settlement and eager to support other Marxist revolutions, Hanoi aided Communist movements in southern Vietnam, Laos, and Cambodia, thus launching the Second Indochina War (1955–1975). By the early 1960s, Hanoi was running a widespread insurgency against the anti-Communist regime in Saigon and aided the Khmer Communists. The Vietnamese Communist leadership ran supply lines to the south through neighboring Lao and Cambodian territory, creating the famous Ho Chi Minh Trail in sparsely populated mountains and jungles. The North Vietnamese decision to move through these two allegedly neutral neighboring countries soon led to the secret and illegal American bombing of first Laos and then Cambodia. These air campaigns failed to break the Ho Chi Minh Trail but inflicted massive collateral damage on the rural civilian population.

In 1955, King Sihanouk abdicated the throne to enter politics. With the title Prince Sihanouk, he became the Kingdom of Cambodia's head of state. 1955 to 1970 is known as the Sangkum Period, as his Sangkum Reastr Niyum (the Popular Socialist Community) dominated the political scene. Despite his charm and charisma, Sihanouk brooked no dissent. Annoyed by the tiny Communist factions, he drove them out of Phnom Penh and into remote rural provinces. These elite Paris-educated Marxists suddenly found themselves living amongst desperately poor farmers. While some perished, others engaged Maoist tactics and ideology to foster a peasant revolution. Yet, Sihanouk, always politically minded, allowed prominent Communist figures such as Khieu Samphan, Hou Yuon, and Hu Nim to enter his government. Dedicated to keeping himself in power, Sihanouk was more than willing to form alliances with whoever could serve his immediate agenda. Thus, he worked with both Marxists and staunch anti-Communists such as General Lon Nol. Sangkum ideology claimed to be "Buddhist Socialist." In reality, it was conservative, nationalist, and monarchist. In international affairs, the prince pursued a stated policy of neutrality during the Cold War, but he was increasingly alarmed by American intervention in Southeast Asia. He thus turned a blind eye to Vietnamese Communists operating the Ho Chi Minh Trail in Cambodia's jungles and mountains. He took things a step further in the mid-1960s when he negotiated a secret deal whereby Hanoi could run supplies through Cambodian ports and stage cross border attacks in the lower Mekong Basin in return for buying Cambodian rice.

Fancying himself a patron of the arts who wanted Cambodians to be proud of their newly independent county, Sihanouk sponsored Khmer cultural projects and funded monumental construction such as Vann Molyvann's Chaktomuk Conference Hall and his Olympic Stadium complex. Some of Oum Ry's most famous fights took place in this impressive sports complex. The prince himself loved to play the saxophone and began to direct locally produced films. For city dwellers with some cash in their pockets, it was a golden age. As Oum Ry recalls, Phnom Penh developed a lively urban culture with bars and discotheques, and even a thriving psychedelic rock scene (seen in the 2014 film *Don't Think I've Forgotten*). Yet there was growing frustration with the regime's anti-democratic nature, Sihanouk's network of cronies, and endemic corruption. If the city's youth were having a good time, many peasants were increasingly desperate. They resented government land-seizures, received below market payments for their rice production, and suffered abuses at the hands of the regime's soldiers. Villagers also resented the arrogance of wealthy city-folk who looked down on them. An increase in urban prostitution was directly tied to girls from poor families being trafficked to Phnom Penh. Oum Ry alludes to the sex trade in his memoir. Despite the bright lights of the big city, most of Cambodia was entering into a serious socio-economic crisis. The one-time Parisian students who led the Khmer Rouge saw an opportunity to put their interpretation of Marxism into action.

In April 1967, the Samlaut Uprising broke out in several provinces. Initially a spontaneous local movement, a faction of the Communist leadership decided to take advantage of the revolt. Sihanouk's Prime Minister and former Minister of Defense, General Lon Nol, savagely cracked down on the revolt. In addition to summary executions and the burning of villages, there were reports of truckloads of severed heads bound for Phnom Penh. Allegedly, Lon Nol offered a bounty for these grisly war trophies. In the chaos, many villagers fled into the jungles and joined the rebels. As the revolt dragged on into 1968, the Khmer Rouge began to launch more organized attacks, leading to the air force bombing rebel bases with significant collateral damage. While the revolt was crushed by April 8, 1968, the government's heavy-handed tactics served as a recruiting tool for the Khmer Rouge. Indeed, the Samlaut Uprising is widely considered the start of the Cambodian Civil War (1967–1968).

During the next two years, right-wing politicians and officers grew increasingly frustrated with Sihanouk, leading to a coup. Lon Nol, Prime Minister and a staunch nationalist and anti-Communist, was infuriated by the idea of Vietnamese Communists on Khmer soil. The right-wingers made common cause with liberal moderates who disliked Sihanouk's authoritarianism. In March 1970, tens of thousands of youths marched on the National Assembly to protest the Vietnamese presence. Within a few days, Prime Minister Lon Nol and Deputy Prime Minister Sirik Matak (a cousin of Prince Sihanouk) seized power and declared an end to the monarchy. They ordered all Vietnamese forces out of Cambodia. This led to attacks on ethnic Vietnamese living in Cambodia, including a massacre in Chroy Changvar, just upstream from Phnom Penh. Some eight hundred ethnic Vietnamese were rounded up, tied together, and killed. Their bodies, some of which were beheaded, were dumped into the Tonle Sap River and later found floating in the Mekong. In 1970, there were close to half a million Vietnamese in the country. However, after three hundred thousand fled or were forced into Vietnam, that population was dramatically reduced. Between the massacres and the ethnic cleansing, one can argue that the Lon Nol regime was guilty of genocide years before the Khmer Rouge seized Phnom Penh. Meanwhile, Lon Nol recruited tens of thousands of civilian men into the army. Oum Ry recounts how, at the height of his career, all sports were shut down and he was forced into the military. Yet he notes that he was not bothered by this as he wanted to defend Cambodia from the Vietnamese.

The 1970 coup had a significant international impact. With the Second Indochina War by this point dragging into its fifteenth year, Henry Kissinger, the American Secretary of State, was surprised by the coup. While there is no direct evidence that the CIA was behind the plot, it seems likely that intelligence agents knew it was coming. Regardless, Washington supported Lon Nol's fierce anti-Communism and Nixon extended military aid to the regime. Hanoi disapproved and Nuon Chea, a high-ranking Khmer Rouge official who would later be known as Brother Number Two, convinced the North Vietnamese regime to invade Cambodia, allowing the Khmer Rouge to spread into new areas. Meanwhile, Prince Sihanouk formed a government in exile in Beijing, the Royal Government of the National Union of Kampuchea, known as GRUNK. Sihanouk also forged an alliance with the Khmer Rouge leadership with most of the top GRUNK positions staffed by Communists. Many peasants rallied to Sihanouk while increasingly violent anti-Lon

Nol protests spread through provincial towns, including a riot in which Lon Nol's brother was murdered. The new Cambodian head of state responded with force and savagely repressed the opposition.

If the initial shots of the Cambodian Civil War were in the Samlaut Uprising, the 1970 coup dramatically escalated the fighting. While North Vietnam's invasion was significant, American involvement increased the violence and destruction. In late April and May 1970, America and South Vietnam invaded eastern Cambodia in a failed effort to find the Vietnamese Communist base of operations. The invasion of neutral Cambodia angered the American public, leading to a series of protests including the deadly demonstration at Kent State in which the Ohio National Guard killed four students. The impact of the American invasion on the Khmer civilian population was devastating; yet this was nothing compared to the toll of the American bombing missions. Started in secret in 1969 as Operation Menu, the Nixon administration illegally bombed significant portions of Cambodia in a failed effort to break the Ho Chi Minh Trail. As the civil war between Lon Nol and the Khmer Rouge heated up, the United States launched Operation Freedom Deal in support of the anti-Communist government. The primary goal was to prevent the encirclement and fall of the capital. In this regard, the three-year campaign was a success. However, as aerial bombardment is an imprecise tool and as rural Cambodia is not a target-rich environment, there was massive collateral damage and civilian casualties. With their villages destroyed, hundreds of thousands of traumatized peasants fled to the safety of the capital city. Soon Phnom Penh was overwhelmed with refugees as close to a third of the nation's population was displaced as a collateral result of the Second Indochina War.

With the Cambodian Civil War continuing, the Cambodian Communist movement steadily grew. American bombing was excellent propaganda for Khmer Rouge recruiters. The party's membership grew dramatically. Many rural Khmer, who were generally conservative and religious, were drawn to the GRUNK out of a reverence for Sihanouk. From 1970 to early 1973, the prince lived in China and North Korea but in February 1973, he flew to Hanoi. There he joined Khieu Samphan and other Khmer Rouge leaders on a journey down the Ho Chi Minh Trail and into Cambodia. Sihanouk braved the American bombs and traveled through the rebel-held northern provinces to visit Angkor Wat, giving credibility to the Khmer Rouge. Others were motivated to join the rebellion by the brutality of Lon Nol's troops and memories of his role in the 1967–1968 violence. The American bombardment completely destabilized Cambodia's economy, creating a population so traumatized that they would be willing to follow the increasingly radical Khmer Rouge. Some argue that this chaos was the only context in which the fringe Marxist movement could have come to power.

The American bombing campaign also changed the Khmer Rouge from its roots as Paris-educated intellectuals, from relatively elite families. Moderates were marginalized, removed, or radicalized. To survive, party leaders adopted a zealous commitment to the revolutionary cause, enforced strict operational secrecy, and delivered brutal discipline. While they were using Lenin's proven tactics for surviving in the political underground, the increasingly bloody civil war pushed the Khmer Rouge into a reign of terror in territory they controlled. The party, which went by the mysterious name of Angkar or "Organization," appealed to the rural masses with promises of revenge against the city dwellers and other elites. Angkar claimed to represent the "Base People," the peasantry, and argued that the "New People" in Phnom Penh were not authentically Khmer. City life had corrupted them from their roots. The revolution would put the Base People on top, or so Angkar promised.

Despite the ferocity of the American bombings, the Lon Nol government steadily lost control of Cambodia. As Nixon withdrew American troops from South Vietnam in January 1973, Operation Freedom Deal continued until August. The increasing distraction of the Watergate scandal, followed by Nixon's August 1974 resignation, and Gerald Ford's unwillingness to return Americans to fighting in Southeast Asia meant that despite public commitments to both Lon Nol and the anti-Communist South Vietnamese government, the Americans did not intervene in 1975. In March and April, the North Vietnamese began an offensive which saw the southern government quickly collapse. Saigon fell on April 30. Meanwhile, the Khmer Rouge, who were increasingly at

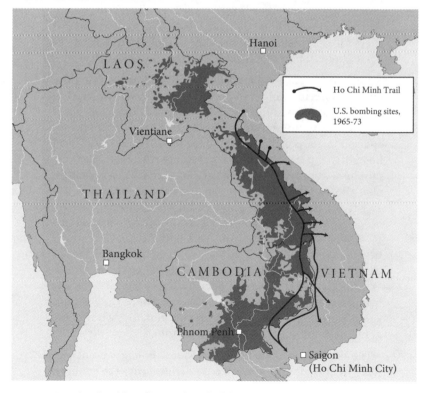

American bombing of Laos and Cambodia, two neutral countries, 1964–1975.

odds with their supposed Vietnamese allies, rushed their assault on Phnom Penh, capturing the city on April 17.

April 17, 1975, is one of the most important dates in Cambodian history. As the insurgents entered Phnom Penh, many residents felt a sense of relief and hoped the awful civil war was over. Many were curious to see what the mysterious Khmer Rouge looked like. Yet the city plunged into chaos. Fearful of reprisals, Lon Nol's troops shed their uniforms and tried to blend in with the civilians. Soon the city's streets were full of guerilla fighters, many of them young peasant boys dressed in black with red scarves wrapped around their necks, heads full of Khmer Rouge propaganda, and crude revolutionary slogans on their lips. They waved their AK-47s, pistols, and grenade launchers to both celebrate their victory and intimidate the conquered city.

As Oum Ry relates, the Khmer Rouge announced that the city, which had swollen to perhaps as many as two million people, had to be immediately evacuated as the Americans were going to bomb Phnom Penh. This was a ruse. In the space of a couple of days, the once bustling capital would be lightly repopulated by Khmer Rouge officials, but their numbers were only in the tens of thousands. The evacuation also allowed the Khmer Rouge to find their enemies, the so-called "New People." They seized government officials, officers, rank-and-file soldiers, and anyone who looked like members of the educated and/or wealthy elite. Executions began immediately. Victims were dragged behind bushes or clumps of bamboo and murdered. Thus began the infamous "killing fields." Chaos reigned as refugees filled the roads leading out of Phnom Penh unclear of where they should go. Fearful of the black clad young men and boys who hurled abuse at them, they did as they were told.

The experience of life under the Khmer Rouge was not uniform. While conditions were truly awful across the country, some zones were safer and quieter than others. As Oum Ry's story shows, an individual's fate was determined by luck and chance as much as it was by cunning and struggle. Some bounced from village to village looking for shelter and food. Others were marched towards rural camps. Eventually, the countryside was dotted with thousands of village communes where the Khmer Rouge tried to enact its dream of an agrarian communist revolution. Private property was outlawed. Everyone was forced to wear dark clothing. Meals were eaten in communal dining areas. Bewildered Cambodians were sat through mandatory political education meetings and chanted Angkar's slogans. New People, also called April 17th People, received the worst treatment and were often worked to death. While some families might be able to live together, others were forced into barracks-like structures. Children received special attention as the Khmer Rouge sought to severe family ties and recruit child soldiers for the revolution. Cadres from Angkar ordered people to work in rice fields or labor on building projects. Due to mismanagement and incompetence, the economy collapsed. Hundreds of thousands died from malnutrition and disease. Improvised medical care was often dangerous and could cause secondary infections.

The Khmer Rouge combined their radical interpretation of Marxism with a rabid nationalism. Despite having previously worked with the Vietnamese communists, they turned on both ethnic Vietnamese in Cambodia and on the newly united Vietnamese nation-state to the east. In a process that began under Lon Nol, thousands of Vietnamese were murdered. The Muslim Cham minority was also subject to violent repression. The ethnic cleansing of Vietnamese and Chams were clear acts of genocide. The Khmer Rouge leaders dreamed of reviving the historic Khmer Empire. As they wanted to control Angkor's former territory, they began to make plans to invade the lower Mekong Delta, which had been part of Vietnamese territory for centuries at this point, conducting a series of quixotic cross border raids.

Meanwhile, increasingly paranoid party officials looked for enemies. The so-called New People were the most obvious targets, but no one was above suspicion. Summary executions were common. As bullets were scarce, prisoners were beaten to death with farm tools or suffocated with plastic bags. In addition, the party turned on itself. As Oum Ry notes, power struggles amongst Khmer Rouge officials turned into deadly conspiracies, blood feuds, and secret purges. A high school in Phnom Penh was repurposed as an interrogation center for high-ranking prisoners. Some fifteen thousand people (overwhelmingly Khmer Rouge cadre) passed through S-21, also known as Tuol Sleng, where they were brutally tortured, forced to sign increasingly absurd "confessions," and then executed in at the Choeung Ek killing fields outside the city. As conditions worsened across Cambodia, irrational violence and mass arrests became more common. Unhinged party officials imagined outlandish plots where the American CIA and the Soviet KGB teamed up with Vietnamese agents and Khmer counterrevolutionaries. The S-21 archives are full of these so-called confessions.

Seeing the revolution fall into insanity and fearful for their own lives, some party members living near the border with Vietnam decided to flee. One of these was a battalion commander named Hun Sen. Having joined the Khmer Rouge in 1970, he had years of military and political service to the party. However, in 1977, he led a small group into Vietnam where he urged the government to intervene in Cambodia. In response to the Khmer Rouge attacks and the genocide against ethnic Vietnamese, Vietnam sent one hundred and fifty thousand troops into Cambodia on December 25, 1978. While the massive Vietnamese army was the core of the invasion, Hun Sen commanded a small unit of ethnic Cambodians. Within days, eastern Cambodia fell to the Vietnamese. Pol Pot and the Khmer Rouge leadership ordered a second evacuation of Phnom Penh. On January 7,

1979, the Vietnamese entered the capital city. Discovering evidence of the Khmer Rouge genocide, the Vietnamese immediately publicized these crimes against humanity. The occupiers quickly turned Tuol Sleng into a museum and the Choeung Ek killing field into a memorial. The Vietnamese established the People's Republic of Kampuchea to replace the Khmer Rouge regime. This puppet government was staffed with Khmer Rouge defectors such as Hun Sen, who at age twenty-six became the Minister of Foreign Affairs. In 1985, Hun Sen became Prime Minister and has held onto to power ever since, making him one of the longest serving heads of state in the world. While he began his career as a Communist, Hun Sen now promotes free markets, welcomes foreign investment in private enterprise, and embraces an increasingly conservative Khmer nationalism.

The Vietnamese invasion can be considered the start of the Third Indochina War (1978–1991). After their initial collapse in early 1979, the Khmer Rouge retreated into the hills and countryside to wage a war of resistance against the Vietnamese invaders. From bases on the Thai border, the Khmer Rouge leadership forged an alliance with other political groups opposed to what they deemed a foreign occupation. Thousands of young Cambodians join the Khmer Rouge forces, not out of a commitment to Marxism but out of a sense of patriotic duty and hatred of Vietnam. As Sihanouk supported the movement, many more joined out of respect for the Buddhist monarch. A decade of civil war between the Vietnamese-backed government in Phnom Penh and the coalition of insurgents prolonged Cambodia's suffering. The war followed a pattern of Vietnamese advances during the dry season and rebel gains during the wet season. As the Vietnamese became increasingly frustrated with the flow of guerilla fighters and supplies from across the Thai-Cambodian border, they embarked on the infamous K5 Plan from 1985 to 1989. Known as the "Bamboo Curtain," this was an attempt to block the enemy's supply routes with a series of trenches, barbed wire fences, and mine fields. Almost four hundred thousand Cambodians were forced to labor on this project. Brutal working conditions, poor food rations, and widespread malaria took a heavy toll on the conscripted laborers and increased anti-Vietnamese sentiment. In addition to the human costs, the K5 Plan was an environmental disaster causing deforestation, loss of species, and erosion.

In the 1980s, millions of Chinese or Soviet manufactured land mines were laid across the Cambodian countryside. Often very poorly mapped, these mine fields killed and maimed an unknown number of Cambodian civilians, including farmers and children. Years after the war was over, it was very common to see amputees begging in Siem Reap and Phnom Penh. Today, visitors to the Angkor archeological sites can visit the Cambodia Land Mine Museum run by Aki Ra (a former Khmer Rouge child soldier, he was forced to lay mines by the Vietnamese but then became a de-mining expert after the war). In the chaos of the war, thousands of displaced people filled refugee centers on the Thai border. Oum Ry's memoir details the confusing and desperate conditions in these camps.

To make matters even more complicated, late Cold War politics such as the Sino-Soviet Split shaped and arguably prolonged the Third Indochina War. As Vietnam was wary of its Chinese neighbor, the Communist government in Hanoi sought the support of the Soviet Union, whose military aid was essential in their occupation of Cambodia. In turn, the People's Republic of China, who had long supported the Khmer Rouge, continued to back up Pol Pot's insurgency, even though the horrors of 1975 to 1978 were increasingly well-known. Despite ending the genocide, the United States of America sanctioned Vietnam for the invasion. Aware that the Vietnamese might push into Thailand, the Americans covertly aided the Khmer Rouge. In a move that is difficult to believe, the Americans refused to recognize the new government and the Khmer Rouge represented Cambodia in the United Nations throughout the 1980s. Thus, as with the American bombing in the early 1970s, great-power politics resulted in massive suffering in Cambodia.

Vietnam occupied Cambodia for over a decade. The Hanoi government was surprised by both the negative international reaction and the ability of the Khmer Rouge to rally Cambodians to their cause. With sanctions devastating their economy and having suffered perhaps fifteen thousand casualties and another thirty thousand wounded, the Vietnamese leadership began to look for a way out of Cambodia. Successful negotiations began in 1988, leading to a rapid withdrawl of troops in the summer and fall of 1989. Thus, just as the Berlin Wall came down, Vietnamese forces left Cambodia. A formal peace treaty was signed two years later. While the 1991 Paris Peace Accords finalized the end to Vietnamese occupation, they placed the administration of Cambodia into the hands of the United Nations Transitional Authority in Cambodia (UNTAC). The UNTAC brought in some twenty thousand soldiers, police officers, and civilian administrators from around the world to disarm the various groups, promote human rights, rebuild infrastructure, and prepare for elections in 1993. UNTAC's success is rather debatable. Elections were held in 1993, with Prince Norodom Ranariddh (Sihanouk's son) defeating Hun Sen. Yet Hun Sen protested his loss and threatened to lead a secession of several eastern provinces. Fearing another civil war, the prince agreed to accept him as a co-premier. In 1997, Hun Sen led a coup d'état and assumed complete control. The presence of so many UNTAC soldiers in Phnom Penh caused an increase in prostitution as desperately poor families turned to sex work to survive. In country where condoms were rare and safe sex practices unknown, this led to a HIV/AIDS epidemic.

While the Khmer Rouge continued to control a number of rural provinces in the 1990s, they refused to participate in the 1993 elections. Fighting continued for years, but by 1996 Hun Sen promoted a new policy he called Win-Win. This was essentially an amnesty for Khmer Rouge troops and leaders. Through a combination of counter-insurgency tactics and political maneuvering, unit after unit began to defect. Faced with these desertions, Pol Pot and his inner circle retreated to the Dangrek Mountains on the Thai border. Political infighting intensified with Pol Pot's arrest and trial by some of his closest allies such as Ta Mok, Khieu Samphan, and Nuon Chea. In April 1998, Pol Pot died under uncertain circumstances. It may have been heart failure, but it may have been suicide as he feared being handed over to the United States. In December 1998, Khieu Samphan and Nuon Chea met with Hun Sen and issued an apology for the genocide. A year later, Ta Mok surrendered, and the Khmer Rouge ceased to exist.

While UNTAC had started to move towards trials for the perpetrators of the crimes against humanity under the Khmer Rouge, Hun Sen was unenthusiastic. While some point to the Buddhist sense of forgiveness as a reason, which is certainly at odds with Western conceptions of justice and accountability, there are more persuasive explanations. We must remember that Hun Sen and many members of his government were once members of the Khmer Rouge. A full investigation could discredit high level officials and members of the new elite. Furthermore, the Win-Win policy promised amnesty for those who put down their arms. Nonetheless, in 1997 Hun Sen and the United Nations agreed to establish a special court that would be called Extraordinary Chambers in the Courts of Cambodia (ECCC). It took years for the trials to get going, with judges not sworn in until 2006. In 2007, the head of the S-21 or Toul Sleng prison, Kang Kek Iew (aka Commander Duch) was indicted, but it was not until September 15, 2010, that the much more high-ranking Nuon Chea, Khieu Samphan, Ieng Sary, and Ieng Thirith were indicted. As they were all elderly, only Khieu Samphan, Nuon Chea, and Duch lived to see their guilty verdicts. Many critics find the trials of a handful of octogenarians woefully insufficient.

Decades of war in Cambodia, Laos, and Vietnam produced a massive refugee crisis. Thailand refused to take in Cambodians, leading to a string of refugee camps on the border. At one-point, Thai authorities tried to force thousands back into Cambodia, leading to an unknown number of deaths as confused and frightened children, women, and men stumbled into minefields. Vietnam was more welcoming, allowing over three hundred thousand Cambodians to settle in the country. International aid programs helped tens of thousands to start new lives in Canada, Australia, and France. Over one hundred and fifty thousand Cambodians were resettled in the United States. Oum Ry's trajectory in America is a familiar story. Initially he lived in the Midwest before he made his way to Long Beach, California, to be part of the largest Khmer community outside of Cambodia. While many Cambodian Americans have made new lives for themselves and their families in the United States, most carry the emotional and physical scars of decades of collective trauma.

One final historical note: there is very little definitive proof of the origins of Southeast Asian kickboxing, though there are many competing theories and fierce debates, with each country claiming it to be their own. In Cambodia, the sport of kickboxing is called Pradal Serey, but is also often referred to as Kun Khmer, which is a generic term for all Cambodian fight styles, including the martial art of Bokator. In Thailand, it goes by the name Muay Thai. Neighboring Myanmar has a similar, yet even more brutal, fighting sport called Lithwei, which is bare knuckled and allows head butts. With little evidence to confirm the sport's exact origins, in the late-twentieth century the international sports fans came to know it as Muay Thai. This is a consequence of the Cold War's economic and political impact on Southeast Asia.

164 | I Am Oum Ry

Thailand, unlike its neighbors, escaped devastating wars in the 1960s and '70s. The Thai military and the Thai king formed an alliance with the Bangkok business community to brutally crush left-wing movements and promote capitalist economic development. The anti-Communist regime allowed the American Air Force to run bombing missions in Vietnam, Laos, and Cambodia from Thai airbases such as Udorn, Ubon, and Korat and opened beach resorts such as Pattaya for American troops to enjoy some rest and recreation. In return, the Thai government received substantial American aid and emerged from the Cold War with a relatively strong economy. However, after 1975, American military spending disappeared, so the Thai government promoted tourism by financing projects to advertise Thai culture. This included investment in Muay Thai as a national sport. By the early twenty-first century, many otherwise well-educated fight fans assume that Muay Thai is the original form of kickboxing and are ignorant of the sport's Khmer roots.

It is important for the reader to note that Pradal Serey and Muay Thai are essentially the same sport with different names and a slightly different scoring system. Many Cambodians are understandably frustrated by what they see as a lack of recognition of their culture's contribution to martial arts.

➤◦➤ Timelines ➤◦➤

802–1431	Khmer Empire
1100s	Angkor Wat built
1177	Cham sack city of Angkor
1295	Theravada Buddhism becomes state religion
1434	Phnom Penh founded
1834–1847	Vietnam occupies most of Cambodia
1841–1845	Siamese-Vietnamese War fought in Cambodia
1863–1953	Cambodge: French Protectorate
1925	Saloth Sar/Pol Pot born

1941–1945	Japanese Occupation of Cambodia during WWII
1946–1954	First Indochina War (France vs. Vietnam)
1951	Communist Party of Kampuchea (Khmer Rouge) founded
1953	Independence from France
1955–1975	Second Indochina War (North Vietnam vs South Vietnam and the United States)
1967–1975	Cambodian Civil War
1969	American bombing begins
1970	Lon Nol coup d'état and American/South Vietnamese invasion
1975–1978	Khmer Rouge takes over Cambodia
1978	Vietnam invades Cambodia
1978–1991	Third Indochina War (Vietnam vs. Cambodia and People's Republic of China)
1979–1989	Vietnamese occupation
1985–present	Hun Sen Prime Minister
1997–present	Trials of the Khmer Rouge happening in Cambodia
1998/1999	Pol Pot dies / Khmer Rouge disbanded

May 15, 1944

Oum Ry is born.

1944–1951

Oum Ry lives / is educated on Koh Chen, an island on the Mekong River.

1951

Oum Ry's grandmother Yeah Puch dies; the family moves from the island.

1952

Oum Ry meets Sarith Ban.

June 1959

Oum Ry enters the monastery in Phnom Penh and begins training.

1960–1975

Oum Ry is continuously a fighter except during 1971 sports program closures.

1966

Oum Pee is born to Oum Ry and Khou Kimny.

1967

Oum Ry becomes Pradal Serey champion of Cambodia after winning against Chea Sarak.

1970–1971

Lon Nol shuts down the sports program for one year starting in April 1970.

1970

Oum Ry joins the army.

July 1972

Oum Ry wins his first International Championship, against Thai fighter Midet Nay.

1970–1974

Oum Ry fights in Cambodia, Thailand, Vietnam, Burma, Malaysia.

February 1975

A baby girl is born to Oum Ry and his wife Pich Dovann.

April 17, 1975

Khmer Rouge invade Phnom Penh and order everyone to evacuate.

1975–1978

Oum Ry and Pich Dovann are forced to farm and labor for the Khmer Rouge; Oum Ry digs graves.

1976

Oum Ry is arrested and put into Kok Trum "celebrity" and government detention center for one month.

mid-1977

Oum Ry escapes forced labor in Phnom Arai.

mid-1977– April 1979

Oum Ry lives on the mountain Phnom Kravanh, becoming de facto leader.

April 1979

Oum Ry escapes capture by Vietnamese soldiers perhaps assuming him to be a rebel with Serey Ka.

April 1979

Oum Ry reunites with his sister Oum Thouk and adopts her son Narith.

July 1979

Oum Ry goes back to Phnom Penh.

1980

Oum Ry meets his future second wife, Yany Sin.

1980 –1981

Oum Ry and Yany live in refugee camps Nong Samet (007) and Khao-I-Dang on the Thai-Cambodian border; Narin is born; relocation to the Philippines.

December 1981–1985

Oum Ry and his family are sponsored by Pastor Stenke and go to live with him in Chicago. Oum Ry learns English working at a hotel and at a casino.

1986–1987

Oum Ry and Yany move to San Jose, California with their children, Narith, Narin, Manila and Unite; Calina is born.

1987

Oum Ry opens his Khmer Kickboxing gym in Long Beach with Paline Soth.

1990

Khmer Kickboxing's first champion, Moun Samath, wins the IKBA title.

1999–2001

Gang intervention program.

2000

Zochada Tat is born to Oum Ry and Socheamony Tat.

November 2006

Gangs attack Oum Ry.

2007

Lifetime Achievement Award from the United Khmer Kickboxing Assoc.

2012

Long Beach Khmer Kickboxing celebrates its twenty-fifth anniversary.

February 2022

Return to Cambodia for workshops and family.

❖ Archive ❖
Photographs and Documents

A rticles, photographs and documents related to the life and times of Oum Ry have been collected by the family, but many more remain lost. For example, there is only one surviving image of the champion Cambodian kickboxer from the 1970s. Documentation showing leadership in the mountains could not be found in time for publication of this book. Certain photographs of champions from the gym are unable to be moved from their locations or properly scanned.

Therefore, the archive on the following pages is necessarily incomplete, but as such, it is a record of what happens to immigrants and refugees when they are forced to leave their homes.

▶ A gate at the Bayon Buddhist temple of Khmer King Jayavarman VII, Angkor Thom in Siem Reap, Cambodia. Angkor Thom is adjacent to Angkor Wat. The Angkor complex of temples remains the largest religious monument on earth, and the Angkor Archaeological Park extends more than four hundred square kilometers, including forested areas and former city capitals (UNESCO). Photo by Chandara Kuon.

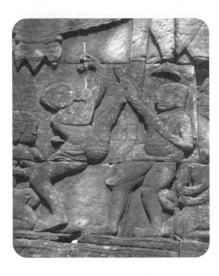

▶ One of the earliest depictions of kickboxing can be found in Siem Reap at the Bayon Buddhist temple, built by the Khmer Emperor Jayavarman VII in the late twelfth and early thirteenth centuries. Photo by Michael G. Vann.

▶ The only known surviving image of Oum Ry during his fighting career prior to the Khmer Rouge takeover — Thai fighter Midet Nay (left) vs. Oum Ry (right) at the Tuol Kouk stadium in 1972 for the International Championship title. Midet Nay threw in the towel during the fifth round, giving Oum Ry the win.

▶ Yany and Oum Ry on the Khmer and Thai border in November of 1979. Yany is about three months pregnant with Narin in this photo.

▶ Oum Ry and son Narin (nicknamed Black Dragon) in a hut at Khao-I-Dang camp. 1980.

▶ Left: Oum Ry and former Pradal Serey fighter Meam Soeun at Khao-I-Dang camp. 1980.

▶ Oum Ry (top row, right) and friends at ESL school in Manila, Philippines. Circa 1981.

▶ Above: Oum Ry and friends after a soccer game at Khao-I-Dang camp. 1980.

▶ Right: Oum Ry's Block Leader certificate from the Refugee Processing Center, Morong, Bataan, Philippines. July 9, 1981.

▶ Below: Oum Ry's Kickboxing Coach training certificate. The course was held August 1980 – January 1981 at Khao-I-Dang camp.

▶ Narin, Oum Ry, Yany, and Manila at their studio apartment in Chicago, Illinois. Circa 1983.

▶ Calina and Unite posing at the gym. 1991.

▶ Don Ban, Narin, Manila, Oum Ry, Yany, Srey Ny, and Bout posing in front of their cars in Chicago, Illinois. 1982.

▶ Oum Ry eating nom pachok (fish noodle soup) at his nephew Nan's house in Long Beach. Circa 1990. Photographed by Yany.

▶ Yany eating nom pachok at Oum Ry's nephew's house. Photographed by Oum Ry.

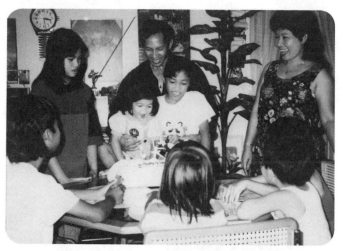

▶ Family celebrating Calina's third birthday in North Long Beach.
  August 23, 1990.

▶ Yany and Oum Ry at San Pedro beach. 1991.

▶ Oum Ry at his gym, Long Beach Khmer Kickboxing. 1991.

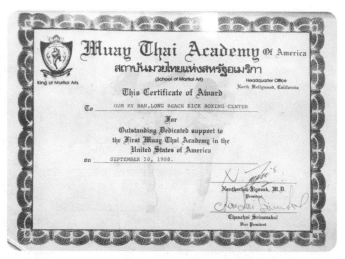

▶ Certificate given to Oum Ry for his outstanding support to the Muay Thai Academy as the first Cambodian gym in the United States and one of the first kickboxing gyms in America. September 10, 1988.

▶ Oum Ry blessing his former kickboxing champion Moun Samat before his fight. 1990.

▶ Oum Ry demonstrating an elbow on former student Marco Morales. 1994.

▶ Students and Oum Ry posing inside the gym's ring. Circa 1990.

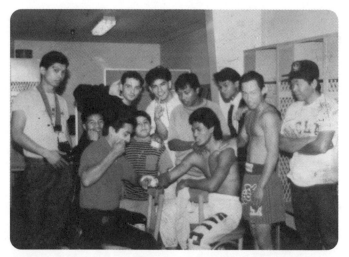

▶ Moun Samat and other Long Beach Khmer Kickboxing students before Samat's fight. 1990.

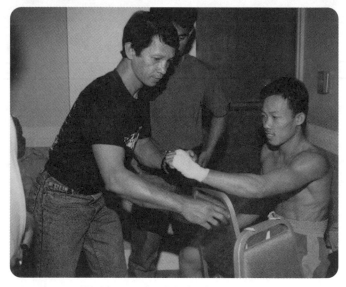

▶ Oum Ry wrapping Pin Karo's hands before his match. 1991.

▶ Oum Ry holding pads as a student throws a right roundhouse kick. 1995.

▶ Bong To, Oum Ry, Sovankesa Som, and Ratha Kalinghanh, photographed after Som's fight in 2016, which he won by unanimous decision. Sovaneska Som is the nephew of Long Beach Khmer Kickboxing's first champion, Moun Samat.

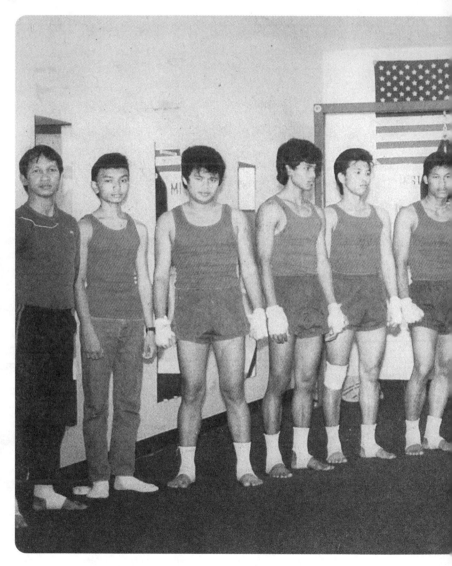

▶ All Cambodian students at Long Beach Khmer Kickboxing
  Center. Circa 1987–88.

▶ Oum Ry and former student and champion Hong Ramya before his fight. 1995.

▶ Lisiate Kapukapu Lavulo, Carlos Garcia, Oum Ry, and Armando Delamora. 1995.

▶ Oum Ry, Marom Marong May, Pros You, and Hong Ramya on the twenty-fifth anniversary commemorative card from Long Beach Khmer Kickboxing. Photo from 1997; card from 2012.

▶ Yany, Manila, Oum Ry, and Unite at a Cambodian Temple in Los Angeles. Circa 1993.

▶ Family day at San Pedro beach. Left to right: Calina, Unite, Oum Ry, Yany, Manila, and Narin. 1991.

▶ Oum Ry's nephew Narith. 1997.

▶ Attending a family friend's wedding. 1993.

▶ Manila, Yany, Calina, Oum Ry, Unite, and Narin at La Lune restaurant in Long Beach. 1995.

▶ Cambodian New Year's celebration (April) with Master Ron Smith (second from right) and students. Circa mid-1990s.

▶ Long Beach Khmer Kickboxing students sparring. Student (left) throwing a sidekick to the inside thigh as student (right) throws a high roundhouse kick. Circa late-1980s.

▶ Advertisement for Long Beach Khmer Kickboxing in the *Khmer Post* from 2009 using photos of Oum Ry from the early 2000s.

▶ Long Beach Khmer Kickboxing students and Oum Ry (middle row, second from left) after a day of training. 1994.

▶ Above: The wall of champions at Long Beach Khmer Kickboxing.
▶ Left: Former IKBA champion, Mao Noth. 2001.

▶ Moun Samat after winning his North American championship title in 1991. (Oum Ry pasted another cut-out photo of him on the front.)

▶ David Woolridge, former Muay Thai champion who trained at Long Beach Khmer Kickboxing. 1997.

▶ Former UKKA champion Long Lorn and Oum Ry, 2004.

▶ Legendary Samoan fighter Sam Moilio in action. 1994.

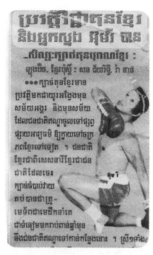

▶ The tiger has remained on the logo for Long Beach Khmer Kickboxing Center throughout its name changes.

▶ "Khmer Martial Arts has a history before the Angkor and before the Indians came to spread civilization.... Khmer people, especially Khmer women, are people who know how to wrestle and fight." *Khmer Post.* Circa 2000s.

▶ Celebratory dinner at Siem Reap restaurant, Long Beach after receiving a Lifetime Achievement Award from the United Khmer Kickboxing Association (UKKA). Oum Ry, third from left, center row. 2007.

▶ Cambodian students and Oum Ry giving a speech at the gang intervention program event in 1999.

▶ Phally Rin, Hong Ramya, and Oum Ry at the gang intervention program event in Long Beach. 1999.

▶ Moun Samat (center, back) and a kids class at Long Beach Khmer Kickboxing. 1993.

▶ Bailey Ban, Unite Ban, Moonney May, and Ruben Gonzales. 1999.

GANG INTERVENTION PROGRAM

OUMRY BAN
Master Trainer

---

223 W. Anaheim St.
Long Beach CA 90813
(562) 591-0533

▶ Brochure from Long Beach Khmer Kickboxing for the Gang Intervention Program run by Oum Ry from 1999–2001 in collaboration with the Department of Parks and Recreation.

GANG INTERVENTION

FIGHTING
FOR PEACE

Eddie Morejon drills at the Long Beach Kickboxing Center.   Ken Kwok / Press-Telegram

Mooney May, 14, right, takes a break as Eddie Morejon practices. They are participating in the Long Beach Kickboxing Gang Intervention Program run by kickboxing champion Oumry Ban.
Ken Kwok / Press-Telegram

Cambodian and Latino youths learn to box, and get along

The sound and smell of sweat and leather...

"Don't slow down now," a young, muscular man in blue shorts and a white tank top exhorts the 10 teens surrounding five heavy punching bags.

"Poomp...poomp," gloved fists sink into stuffed bags, the rhythm occasionally interrupted by an elbow blow. Weary legs are lifted, then quickly snapped into the thick bags.

"Thirty seconds left," the

RALPH DE LA CRUZ

taskmaster yells out. "Pick it up. Pick it up."

"Poomp, poomp, poomp," comes the answer.

Sweat and leather.

For much of our country's

history, boxing gyms have told the story of immigration and the struggle for respect.

Irish, Polish, Jewish, Italian, African-American, Latino and Southeast Asian. An American roll call. Different generations, different people, connected by an underdog's anger and hunger.

By sweat and leather.

It's certainly a story that

PLEASE SEE **SWEAT** / A

▶ *Long Beach Press-Telegram* article on the gang intervention program at Long Beach Khmer Kickboxing run by Oum Ry. Date unknown, circa 2000. Photo by Ken Kwok. Courtesy of Oum Ry's daughter Manila Ban, who saved these clippings.

SWEAT: Kick-boxing works for at-risk youth

applies to our immigrant-laden Southland communities.

But there's a twist to the Long Beach story, circa 1999.

Maybe more like a kick.

"Welcome to the Long Beach Kickboxing Center," reads the skirt wrapped around the bottom of the 16-by-16-foot ring inside the gym at 223 W. Anaheim St.

Or at least that's what Oumry Ban, the ex-professional kickboxer who runs the gym, tells me it says. I have to take his word. It's written in Khmer.

Three flags

One of the walls has three large flags: A large U.S. flag flanked by slightly smaller Cambodian and Mexican flags.

Reminders of the cultural cohesion Ban hopes to create between youngsters.

Since September, Ban has been conducting a program that teaches Khmer kickboxing to Latino and Cambodian youngsters, many of them associated with gangs.

The idea came from Long Beach resident Charlie Wise, a volunteer for the Fulfillment Fund in Los Angeles who was mentoring a Latino youngster who wanted to learn kickboxing.

Wise looked in the Yellow Pages and found Ban's gym. After checking it out, Wise knew it had the potential to unify.

"I thought it would be perfect, since kickboxing is the national sport of Cambodia and Thailand, and boxing's always been big in the Hispanic community," he says.

He formed relationships with the county probation department and the Gang Intervention and Prevention Program of the Long Beach Department of Parks, Recreation and Marine.

Sung Oh, a county probation officer who was with the Asian Gang Task Force, suggested seven Asian teens for the program. The city folks suggested 10 Latinos. Those 17 joined four other teens who were already in Ban's class.

Learning respect

"I can tell you that with this kind of martial art, you have to learn how to respect," says Oh, a Korean who has trained in tae kwon do. "Also, discipline. Also how to be patient.

"Besides the mental part, when you sweat it out in kickboxing, you go home and go to sleep. You don't have the time or energy to get into trouble."

Wise spoke with the office of County Commissioner Don Knabe, which agreed to provide $11,500 to fund the program.

The Long Beach Kickboxing Gang Intervention Program was born.

But that's the always-complicated nuts and bolts aspect of what's happening on West Anaheim.

The sweat-and-leather part is simpler.

"I like to fight with my family," says Kathy Reyes, 17. "But when I train here, I don't really have time for that. I get home, shower, eat and go to sleep. And I've learned how to respect my parents, too."

"It's about anger and control," says Femi Williams, an 18-year-old in another class. "You can vent your anger. But you also have to control it. It makes me strong, makes me quick and makes me more aware of my surroundings. The best part is I lost 15 pounds."

"I come here to develop stamina, endurance and to learn how to defend myself," says Absalon Rosas, 16. "The toughest part? Showing up."

If you haven't figured it out yet, respect is the glue that holds the program together.

Three rules

"I always tell them, 'Listen to parents, number one,' " says Ban. " 'Number two, respect teachers. Number three, respect yourself.' "

"The most important thing is, be respectful," says Marco Morales, one of Ban's trainers. He's the one who'd been pressing the class to "pick it up."

"If they come in and show me

and the other instructors respect, then they'll be able to respect others," Morales says. "If you have respect, everything else – discipline, organization – comes natural."

The philosophy seems to register. The program has been virtually problem-free.

"Five or six months ago, we had a 14-year-old Hispanic kid accidentally kick a 17-year-old Asian," says Wise, recalling a rare tense moment. "Later, the Asian told him, 'You're not showing me any respect. I'm going to deal with you later.' The Hispanic kid told me later what had happened and that he had to quit. I asked, 'Did you apologize?' He said, 'No.' The kid lacked some understanding of basic etiquette."

Wise spoke to the Asian youngster and told him the Latino teen was going to quit.

The Asian teen said he didn't want that to happen. He explained that, in anger, he had spoken to the Latino youngster as if he were talking to his homeboys, and maybe that was wrong."

The next day, the two boys apologized and eventually became friends.

Just a little sweat and leather bringing people together.

Ralph De La Cruz's viewpoint appears Saturdays, Sundays, Mondays and Wednesdays. He may be reached at (562) 499-1302.

The Kickboxer's Tale

A Cambodian champion keeps battling for a better life

By Greg Mellen / Staff writer

This truth a fighter knows: Sometimes the psychological scars are the worst. Bruises subside, cuts close, broken bones heal. But memories, pride, honor — those are things less easily salved.

When one is blind-sided and savagely beaten on the streets of Long Beach, that's tough to reconcile.

When Oumry Ban arises in the hours before dawn, as he does each day, the 63-year-old former Khmer kickboxing champion and Cambodian genocide survivor stares into the bathroom mirror. He traces his hand along his face and feels nothing — literally.

PLEASE SEE **BAN / A12**

MORE ONLINE

At **www.presstelegram.com**, hear Oumry Ban in his own words, learn some key kickboxing moves, and hear one of Oumry's students talk about the man and his gym.

▶ *Long Beach Press-Telegram*, July 1, 2007. The full article is archived at http://www.presstelegram.com/ci_6273151

▶ Article from the *Long Beach Press-Telegram*, July 1, 2007, continued. Seated in the courtroom during the trial (front row) are Oum Ry and his daughter Manila.

▶ "What to think about the tragedy of Master Oum Ry. This past Saturday, November 8, was a painful day. 'The crime was so painful for all of us,' says one of Oum Ry's students. Hundreds of students lined up outside of the gym after the incident...." *Serey Pheap Weekly Cambodian News*. January 29, 2007.

▶ Continuation of the *Serey Pheap Weekly Cambodian News* article, giving a history of the gym and Oum Ry's biography. January 29, 2007.

▶ *Long Beach Press-Telegram* feature article on Oum Ry and Long Beach Khmer Kickboxing with photos taken by Kevin Chang.

▶ Right: Master Ron Smith and Oum Ry in the ring. Opposite page, clockwise from the top: Oum Ry, age sixty-three, Oum Ry and Zochada walking to school, and Oum Ry talking on the phone in their one room apartment. July 1, 2007.

Long Beach, California S U N D A Y , J U L Y 1 , 2 0 0 7 51 (plus

A proud defender of family and sport

Oumry Ban, 63, a former Khmer kickboxing champion and Cambodian genocide survivor, moved to Long Beach to start a new life in 1986 — and then had to start again in November of last year, when a street attack nearly took his life. Above right, Ban walks with his youngest daughter, Sochada Tat, 7, after school one day. At right, Ban relaxes in the one-bedroom apartment he shares with his girlfriend and two daughters. Below right, he jokes with one of his former students, Ron Smith, who is now an instructor teaching Victor Canela, 13, left. Below, Ban blocks a kick from a student during a training session.

▶ Oum Ry holding Zochada. Circa 2000–2001.

▶ Framed photo hanging in the gym of Zochada in Thai boxing shorts. June 22, 2005.

▶ Oum Ry holding Zochada on his shoulder. 2001.

▶ Oum Ry throwing a left knee while Marom Marong May is about to execute a left elbow in the ring at Long Beach Khmer Kickboxing. 2005.

▶ Master Ron Smith, Mony Tat, Oum Ry and Zochada at the gym. Circa 2004.

▶ Zochada standing on a table in the gym's office. Circa 2005.

▶ Zochada and Yany at her home in North Long Beach. 2004.

▶ Zochada and Oum Ry holding his Lifetime Achievement Award from United Khmer Kickboxing Association. 2007.

▶ Zochada trying on Moun Samat's North American championship belt. 2007.

▶ Long Beach Khmer Kickboxing Center. June 2022.

▶ Oum Ry, Bokator master San Kim Sean, Sam Eun, Sarith Ban, and the late
So Costo, another Pradal Serey fighter. Long Beach, California, 2006.

THE WARM-UP DANCE (KUNN-KRU)

Our warm-up dance or (kunn-kru) is a typical khmer-boxing tradition. It display a very tradional role to the boxers as well as the audience. For the boxers it serves as a warm-up and to better condition thier fighting spirit. They will pay homage to their teachers (kunn-kru) and pray for non-injury and good luck in the ring. Every moment of the dance is graceful and beautiful to watch while the arousing music of flutes, drum and cymbals are played. Their style of dancing or (kunn-Kru) are distinguished from camp to camp.

▶ Above: Long Beach Khmer Kickboxing doing an exhibition at The Inosanto Academy of Martial Arts in Marina Del Rey. October 28, 2014.

▶ Left: An old Long Beach Khmer Kickboxing pamphlet that used to be passed out to students, explaining the Twai Kru dance, sometimes also known as Kunn-Kru. 2002.

▶ Master Ron Smith at the gym. 1994.

▶ Certificate of appreciation from Elite Combat Systems. August 2015.

▶ Zochada and Oum Ry on the way to Cambodia. Photo by Frances Weinberg. January 28, 2022.

▶ Oum Ry and a fan in Phnom Penh. February 2022.

▶ Tippana Tith, Addi Somekh, Oum Ry and Zochada in Long Beach Khmer Kickboxing after an interview session. Photo by Ron Smith. 2021.

▶ Oum Ry posing with young fans in front of the Tuol Kouk stadium. February 2022.

▶ Oum Ry watching a live televised Pradal Serey fight at the Tuol Kouk stadium with one of the judges. Phnom Penh, February 10, 2022.

▶ Oum Ry and Chhit Sarim, Pradal Serey masters who survived the Cambodian genocide.

▶ Oum Ry giving a thumbs up on a houseboat floating on the Tonle Sap River.

▶ Oum Pee, Srey Pich and her daughter, Zochada and Oum Ry meet for the first time in Oum Pee's hometown Kampong Chham. February 2, 2022.

▶ Oum Ry meeting some of his great grandchildren for the first time at Darasy Oum's house in Phnom Penh. February 21, 2022.

▶ Oum Ry getting interviewed by three Cambodian national news channels. February 10, 2022.

▶ Oum Ry's official visit with the government Ministry of Sport. February 10, 2022.

▶ Oum Ry posing with Pradal Serey fighters at the KTV studio. February 10, 2022.

▶ Oum Ry and Chhit Sarim with Pradal Serey fighters at the Tuol Kouk stadium. February 8, 2022.

▶ Oum Ry and lead instructor Sarak Plive demonstrating an outside kick at Kingdom Fight Gym in Siem Reap. February 12, 2022.

▶ Chhit Sarim and Oum Ry getting interviewed on stage by Bayon TV. February 20, 2022.

▶ Oum Ry and a fan. February 2022.

▶ Oum Ry is about to demonstrate a Pradal Serey technique on Sarak
 Plive, one of the head instructors at Kingdom Fight Gym in Siem Reap.
 February 12, 2022.

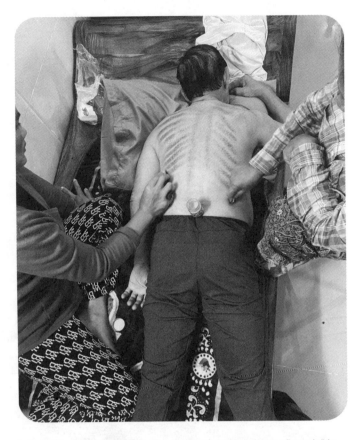

▶ Oum Ry getting "coined" by family members. Coining, or "cao gio" in
Khmer, is a common Southeast Asian remedy for minor illnesses such
as cold, runny nose, headache, fever, pain, cough, or low energy. Coining
is performed by lubricating the skin with an ointment like Tiger Balm
and then taking a hard metal object, most often a coin or a spoon, and
rubbing it along the skin of the back, neck, shoulder and chest until a
bruise is present. It is similar to dermabrasion in Western medicine
or cupping in Chinese medicine. The theory behind coining is that it
promotes blood flow and releases toxins from the body, thus restoring
proper health. While the bruising usually lasts three days, people claim
to feel instant relief. A common saying in the Cambodian community is,
"Why go to a doctor when you can get coined at home?"

▶ Oum Ry visiting Angkor Wat for the first time and feeling invigorated. February 12, 2022.

▶ Family photo at Angkor Wat. Left to right: Vichet So, Chantra Oum, Vireak, Sreynak Um, Oum Ry, Darasy Oum, and Zochada. February 12, 2022.

⟣ Acknowledgments ⟣
by Zochada Tat

There are many people to thank for extending support to my dad and I in order to realize this book. I am immeasurably grateful for you all. Not only has this project made the bond between my dad and I greater, it has also brought me closer to all of you. To my fellow Cambodians — I hope this book will give you some insight into the relationships around you. I hope you're able to find peace.

Yany Sin — You are the most resilient person I know, and I appreciate everything you do for everyone.

Tippana Tith — Thank you so much for coming to every interview and helping with the translation. Your expertise and dedication have been invaluable.

Manila Ban — A big thank you to my oldest sister for providing all of the family photos and the articles, and for keeping our father so close.

Special thanks to: Rosemary Ban, Carson Fugate, Calina Sin, Paline Soth, Sarith Ban, Rotpichchan Tha, Moun Samat, Ron Smith, Chhit Sarim, Moonney May, Marom Marong May, Alaysha Sisson, Serena Chea, Bianka Carpio, Yuna Shibata, Taerin Kang, Jess Boyer, Socheamony Tat, Darasy Oum, Miranda Oum, Vichet So, Oum Pee, Kwok-Leung Tsang, Kingdom Fight Gym, Mr. Kun Ly Gym, Sarak Plive, Chum Kolthyda, Rick Leng, An Chhay, Douglas J. Mackinnon, Udom Khmer restaurant, Hak Heang restaurant, and the Cambodian Film Festival.

▶ Oum Ry and Zochada walking down the streets of Phnom Penh.
  February 2022.

To my friend and coauthor, Addi Somekh, this journey has been a ride, and I'm glad that you were sitting shotgun. Warmest thanks to our wonderful publisher, Carrie Paterson, for administering our book and for her astute comments and concerns. It has truly been an honor working with you.

Pa, it's quite impossible to thank you adequately for all that you have done, not only for me, but for anyone else that has been fortunate to cross paths with you. You've instilled in me the importance of health, humility, and having heart in everything that I do. Your golden heart is my favorite thing about you. Kuon sraleanh, Pa.

Additional Acknowledgments
by Addi Somekh

I would like to thank: Eta, Sass and Talli Somekh, Gladden Rangel, Sailin Nelson, Eddie "Tiny" Michael and Marco Huerta at the Old Town Pub, Alan Christy and Cowell College at UC Santa Cruz, Michael G. Vann, Brian Knappmiller, Christine Ventenilla, James Borrelli, Kathy Rose and Paul Schoellhamer, Wayne Cartwright, Shahin Kianpour, Daniele Bolelli, Alanna Lin, Gustaf Cedermalm, Nathalie Carlón, Greg Mellen, Tom Welsh, Loung Ung, Sophy's on PCH, Magdalena Zucker and Margaret Kilroy for their assistance writing the notes, Joey Maramba and Laila Morris, Tippana Tith for always being there to help, Carrie Paterson for inspiring and guiding this book, and special thanks to Oum Ry and Zochada for trusting me to help tell their story.